Gateshead
Council

CW00968677

Due for Return	Due for Return	Due for Return

Visit us at:

www.gateshead.gov.uk/books

Tel: 0191 433 8410

trichotillomania, dermatillomania and RSS, a condition she suffered from for over two years. She has since made a full recovery and is an advocate for the relatively unknown condition, which affects thousands of people ....alise living with a me ...nt in our society to

C1 940473 60

First published in Great Britain 2018 by Trigger

Trigger is a trading style of Shaw Callaghan Ltd & Shaw Callaghan 23 USA, INC.

The Foundation Centre

Navigation House, 48 Millgate, Newark

Nottinghamshire NG24 4TS UK

www.triggerpublishing.com

Copyright © Cara Ward 2018

British Library Cataloguing in Publication Data

A CIP catalogue record for this book is available upon request
from the British Library

ISBN: 978-1-912478-30-9

This book is also available in the following e-Book and Audio formats:

MOBI: 978-1-912478-33-0
EPUB: 978-1-912478-31-6
PDF: 978-1-912478-32-3
AUDIO: 978-1-78956-050-3

Cara Ward has asserted her right under the Copyright,
Design and Patents Act 1988 to be identified as the author of this work

Cover design and typeset by Fusion Graphic Design Ltd

Printed and bound in Great Britain by Clays Ltd, Elcograf S.p.A

Paper from responsible sources

www.triggerpublishing.com

Thank you for purchasing this book.
You are making an incredible difference.

Proceeds from all Trigger books go directly to
The Shaw Mind Foundation, a global charity that focuses
entirely on mental health. To find out more about
The Shaw Mind Foundation visit,
www.shawmindfoundation.org

MISSION STATEMENT

Our goal is to make help and support available for every
single person in society, from all walks of life.
We will never stop offering hope. These are our promises.

Trigger and The Shaw Mind Foundation

TThe Inspirational range from Trigger brings you genuine stories about our authors' experiences with mental health problems.

Some of the stories in our Inspirational range will move you to tears. Some will make you laugh. Some will make you feel angry, or surprised, or uplifted. Hopefully they will all change the way you see mental health problems.

These are stories we can all relate to and engage with. Stories of people experiencing mental health difficulties and finding their own ways to overcome them with dignity, humour, perseverance and spirit.

Skin picking and hair pulling disorders are not well publicised or discussed, despite affecting a large number of people. Cara's story is an honest account of a problem that left her ashamed, embarrassed and, at times, housebound. She showed strength and determination to overcome these difficulties, and by sharing her diary excerpts, Cara shows humour and dignity in dealing with very emotional and physically difficult experiences. Her honesty about her journey and eventual recovery provides hope and inspiration for others.

This is our Inspirational range. These are our stories. We hope you enjoy them. And most of all, we hope that they will educate and inspire you. That's what this range is all about.

Lauren Callaghan

To RSS, the condition that changed my life and made me believe anything was possible, including this book.

Disclaimer: Some names and identifying details have been changed to protect the privacy of individuals.

Trigger Warning: This book contains references to, and accounts of, hair pulling disorder (trichotillomania) and skin picking disorder (dermatillomania).

AUTHOR'S NOTE

This is a graphic account of my battle with trichotillomania and dermatillomania which some readers might find distressing and potentially even a trigger.

This book is not some kind of manual on how to beat these disorders: it is a journal written over seven weeks, during which I finally found a way of managing my compulsions. It also discusses the mental and physical journey I went on during that time. What worked for me might not necessarily work for you – we are all different.

My aim with the book is, of course, to offer help and support to others going through one or both compulsions. But more than anything, I want those who are suffering to not feel so alone – I want you to know that there is nothing wrong with you and you are only human. We are all dealing with something, either mentally or physically, and you are doing the best you can – never forget that.

I truly hope you find this book helpful, but do read with caution as I've held nothing back ... Oh my goodness.

Cara x

CHAPTER 1

CONCEPTION

I think often about how and when this *thing* began. I wonder how trichotillomania and dermatillomania were able to worm themselves into my life and do everything in their power to control me.

My name is Cara Ward, and I was born in London on 29th September 1987. I was a surprisingly small baby considering that I grew up to be six feet tall. I was raised in England's capital by my wonderful mother and grandmother and had what can only be described as a blissful childhood in a time before smartphones and tablets. I was carefree and happy, with only a little bit of mild eczema to concern myself with. My young school life was uncomplicated and free from problems.

I'm not exactly sure when it happened but it was almost innocent in its origins ... At the time I was very unhappy at secondary school – a victim of the dreaded "B" word. I'm still coming to terms with the bullying now. I had just hit puberty – I believe I was about 12, maybe 13 years old – and had started getting hair under my arms. My mum let me use her electric shaver to get rid of it, but afterwards I noticed a hair that hadn't been picked up. I thought it would be okay to just pull it out with the tweezers.

That innocent action cost me over 16 years of my life.

I imagine it's hard to understand how the simple act of pulling just one hair can lead to a problem, especially one that took over so much of my life. But when something begins as a small, insignificant thing – a harmless action that you don't even understand yourself – a smart compulsion like trichotillomania can latch onto your ignorance and only educate you when it is too late.

At first, you think you are only pulling hairs for vanity's sake, until suddenly you are mostly doing it because you *like* it – and that is when you realise you have a problem.

Back then, it felt like I had a thirst that could only be quenched by pulling. But still, even when I first knew I had a problem, I didn't think about what *could* happen in the future. I only thought of the now. I understood it enough to know that I liked doing it. I found it to be a release against the pressures of school, and at the time I didn't contemplate stopping, because I was so desperately in need of something that would help me escape from my reality. I wanted a distraction from school and how that experience made me feel both mentally and physically.

At the beginning it was very much an experiment and I trialled out what I did and didn't like. Now, if I could meet my very scared 12-year-old self, I would put my arms around her and tell her to seek help before the trich grows into a beast.

But I can't; here we are, many years later, and I'm writing a book on the very subject.

There is a thick mist shrouded over the first phase of my life with trichotillomania, as it's so long ago now. I know some of my memories of the condition will be deeply etched into my mind for the rest of my life, but others are hazy and waiting to be explored.

For a while, I was able to contain the problem to under my arms. But as the compulsion grew stronger (and let's be real, I probably ran out of hairs to pull out), I moved on to my eyebrows.

My legs got involved after that, followed by my bikini line. Then my breasts. My beef against lone, stray dark hairs on my stomach began only a few years ago.

Trichotillomania is most commonly associated with pulling out the hair on your head. But oddly, I've never felt any compulsion to do that. Maybe it's because deep down I know that if I did that, everyone would know I had a problem. And I wouldn't want *that* – heaven forbid!

If someone said to me right now, 'Pick a compulsion you have suffered from the most: trichotillomania or dermatillomania', the answer would be a no-brainer. It's trich. That was the compulsion I started with, and that's the one that has been the most prevalent in my life.

I believe that dermatillomania was, for me at least, a direct result and by-product of my trichotillomania, because sometimes, in order to get a hair out, you have to pick at your skin. That is why this book is predominantly focused on my battle with hair pulling. That doesn't mean derma hasn't had a knock-on effect on my life. But for now, I think it's important to concentrate on the hair pulling.

One of my earliest memories of trichotillomania was when I was watching a film. I think I must have been about 13 years old. As I watched, I looked down absent-mindedly and noticed I had an ingrown hair. It was in my right armpit and it must have been a centimetre in length. It was lying flat against my skin, almost as if it was a running stitch.

To this day it's the most beautiful ingrown hair I've ever seen.

If you suffer from trichotillomania, you will appreciate there is a kind of beauty to hair. Each and every single strand is different and exciting. They trigger certain emotions and feelings inside you, as if they were a person.

I can't lie – I was beyond excited to tackle it, so I secretly got my mum's cuticle clippers (I know) and used one of its razor-sharp ends to pierce the skin, hooking out the hair. This hair kept coming out of my skin like it was a magic trick, and for years

I waited for another ingrown hair to reappear there, but it never did. For the first few years I was pretty much obsessed with the hair under my arms, and I did some damage that I'm definitely not proud of.

Most people wouldn't even dream that this part of me even existed, but like most people suffering from trichotillomania and / or dermatillomania, I am an expert at deception. It's strange how isolating and secretive we all tend to be about our compulsions. There is an embarrassment, a feeling of shame, which comes as part and parcel of our disorders. We have compulsions that should be within our power to control, but they're impossible to resist. We should be masters of our own destinies and be able to do whatever we tell ourselves to do, and yet some of us just can't stop touching our skin and hair.

These disorders can stop you from living your life. They can change your plans and stop you from dating, going out or seeing friends. It's a terrible realisation knowing that the thing you want most is within your grasp physically, but mentally you are powerless.

There was a period – about seven years ago, maybe – when I had a job that I hated. It made me feel like I was melting with boredom. At work I got into the habit of "de-clumping" my mascara so that it was nice and smooth, but before I knew it, my eyelashes were thin on the ground. I think that is the only area of my body where I acknowledged that I *might* have had the beginnings of a problem, and I stopped before it was too late. I remember it was hard to quit, but not impossible. My eyelashes grew back (and I handed in my notice!).

I think my own personal experience of living with the compulsion – teamed with a hefty amount of hindsight – was beneficial to me when it came to my eyelashes. I had accepted many years earlier that I had a pretty serious problem. It was almost as if it was too late to stop with other areas of my body, as I had been attacking them for a long time; whereas with my eyelashes, the sensation of pulling there was new. I hadn't let it become part of my routine yet. As a behaviour, it was still in the early stages and it hadn't become a habit. It's similar to dating a man and leaving before letting my feelings for him turn into something deeper, more meaningful.

My mum is the only person who has ever really known I had a problem. Years ago, she walked in on me picking and pulling under my arms. She was shocked. She couldn't understand why I was doing it. But over the years she has tried her best to understand the daughter who doesn't even understand herself. With only my mum in on my dirty little secret, I told no one – even my closest friends were none the wiser.

I feared people's reactions to something I didn't even fully understand myself. The chance of possible rejection from others terrified me. I believed that those who knew me wouldn't accept it, because I didn't accept it myself.

Marks made as a result of both compulsions were explained away as acne (that I didn't have), razor bumps, eczema ... the list is endless. If you have trichotillomania or dermatillomania, it's likely you will have a book full of excuses and explanations, ready to offer those who suspect that something is not what it seems.

Even though I knew I had a problem, I never thought to seek medical help or go to the doctor about my disorders. I was simply too embarrassed; it made me feel dirty, weak and helpless. I couldn't stop, and I didn't think anyone else would have what I have. My mum pleaded with me to get help, but I couldn't.

It's odd, the moment you find the name for your compulsions. Even when I learnt that they are actual mental disorders recognised by the medical community, I still couldn't put two and two together and realise that others had them too.

I found the name for my condition after becoming more curious than anything else. I wondered whether some small part of the World Wide Web knew my dirty little secret. I have a memory of feeling completely numb upon seeing the word

T-r-i-c-h-o-t-i-l-l-o-m-a-n-i-a

for the first time. It's such a long and complicated word, so much like the compulsion itself.

You would think that finding the word would be this hallelujah moment for any sufferer. Perhaps you'd think it's a feeling of validation, almost as if you were part of this new and exclusive club. But I just felt alone. Having a compulsion like trichotillomania and / or dermatillomania can be incredibly isolating and even after seeing the name for the first time, it didn't truly convince me that others had it. I know, strange, but the mind works in mysterious ways and all we can do is accept this and try to hang on tight to the roller coaster that is life.

These disorders affected me not only physically, but also mentally. I truly believe they changed the course of my life – who knows what would have happened if I hadn't suffered from these compulsions.

I could be married right now. I spent too many years running from all opportunities with the opposite sex because I was too nervous to show my naked, marked flesh to another person. I feared their rejection.

I could have had a successful career, but suffering from trich can pull you down, make you think less of yourself and stop you from going for what you really want. The belief you hold in yourself is about as small as you feel.

I wasted so many hours in the bathroom, picking at my skin. At my worst, I'd lock myself in the bathroom for hours on end and mercilessly pick, gouge and pull at my skin. Then, along with the shame and regret, out would come the antiseptic.

So many times I didn't go out, because I'd picked past the point of no return and was literally too scared to show my face, which was littered with gouges.

I missed so many auditions when I was trying to become a performer; I missed one because I needed to wear a skirt, and another because it called for the lead actor to swim. I couldn't do either of those things with my legs.

If you have suffered with trich and derma for as long as I have, then you will be very aware of the risk you are taking with your skin. The chances of getting an infection – which I have *somehow* evaded for so long – are sky high. As a result, you will need to take precautions seriously, as having that much open skin is just asking for trouble. Antiseptic is a truly brilliant thing but the smell isn't – and this is highly inconvenient when you have a compulsion you are trying to keep a secret.

My mum always knew when I had been picking. Sometimes, I would emerge from the bathroom and she'd ask me, 'Have you been picking, Cara?'

I'd give a small, sheepish, 'No', my answer completely negated by the antiseptic smell surrounding me like a force field.

There was a time when I was much older – maybe in my early to mid-twenties – where I'd spent hours really attacking my legs. I had plans with a group of friends that evening, but because I had taken so long, I was left with very little time to get ready. Even though my legs were a complete mess – really quite scary, even by my standards – I wanted to wear a dress. So, I covered my deepest, darkest secret with thick black tights.

On the Tube on the way to the party, my legs were in serious pain. And no wonder, seeing as they were completely covered in deep, open wounds. I looked down and saw the dark shadows of blood through my tights. Because I was in a rush before I left – and because I didn't want to smell like a pharmacy – I hadn't used antiseptic. I was more scared than I've ever been that I'd caught a serious infection and I spent the whole night trying to work out whether I needed to go to A&E, or if I should just ignore it.

I ignored it and had the worst time of my life. But to everyone else, I appeared to be having a *fabulous* time.

No one must ever know about my dirty little secret.

I stayed over at my friend's house, but I definitely didn't want my friend to see my legs in that state. I feigned being cold as I was too scared to take off my tights and look at them.

The following day, when I got back home and tried to take off my tights, I couldn't get them past my knees. They had completely stuck to my legs.

The fabric had welded to my dried blood, so I had to get in the shower, put warm water over my legs and gradually unstick my tights as the blood loosened. Afterwards, I sat in that bathroom and – for the first time ever – I really forced myself to look at my legs. It was horrific. There were still bits from my black tights trapped in some of the wounds, and I also had these dark red holes all over my skin. It was a moment as dark as my blood-spattered legs.

What the hell are you doing, Cara? I thought to myself.

At that moment I made what I thought was a solemn vow to stop picking, right there and then. I wanted to turn my life around. But of course, I broke my empty promise and lasted maybe a day before I was back picking my legs. The fear and desperate sadness I'd experienced in that bathroom was forgotten.

But since that day, I've never gone back to *that* place. And I know, no matter what, that I never will again.

I know it's not exactly a story to feel proud of, but I think before I leave all this behind, I want an account of everything I have done to myself because of trich and derma. No matter what, it's still something that was a huge part of my life for over 16 years. I have had this memory, and so many others like it, trapped in my head for such a long time, rotting away and I think there is part of me that has been scared to let them out – but now, it's time to move on.

Looking back, I am so happy with how things turned out, but that doesn't mean it's been easy. My twenties were especially tough, and I definitely missed out on a lot of things most women at that time of their life take for granted, like dating. Then again, we live in an age of social media, which skews everything and makes you believe that everyone is having the most amazing time, when we all know that isn't the case.

In this book I will be sharing the life-defining, life-shaping moments that have made up the last 16 years of my life. It will be brutal and painful, but hopefully in the end it will be freeing. Welcome to my mind.

CHAPTER 2

THE TRIGGER

It was school.

Chapter over.

*

Fine, I'll elaborate. But even now, talking about this time of my life is painful, like pulling off an old plaster that's been on too long and now feels bonded to my skin. But I know that if I don't talk about it, I'll never heal. Wounds need time to breathe.

*

School. A word which can evoke such wonderful emotions for some. For others, that simple six-letter word can make you feel like all the light has suddenly gone out, like every bit of happiness you've ever felt is slowly draining out of you. Your formative years are so important; you are a sponge, soaking everything up, and even the smallest thing can have the most devastating impact on your life.

I believe you are born with the desire to pick and pull, but in my case at least I needed a catalyst in order to give it life. Think of the bullying at school – a very stressful situation – as a rich, fertile soil. Trich and derma are the seeds, and once planted, they blossomed into a terrible tree with thick roots and many branches. Each of those branches represents the different ways in which the condition impacted my life.

As an 11-year-old girl taking her first steps into the unknown, I didn't really stand a chance. I was about a foot taller than anyone else, redheaded (because for some reason its socially acceptable to bully those with my heritage) and suffering from eczema. To top it all off, I didn't fight back. There you have the makings of a perfect punch bag.

Back then, it felt like I'd be in school forever, trapped with my bullies for all eternity. I couldn't imagine a life outside the school's oppressive clutches and I was too scared to stand up for myself. I didn't feel like there was a way out. I was very reluctant to tell my mum anything about what was going on, because I knew she would want to tell the school. And besides, when you're in this situation, *you* are the one that has to return to school, no one else. You can't just tell your parents and the school what has happened and then be allowed to vanish into the ether. I knew that if I did anything, I'd have to live with the consequences and see the same people who had tormented me in the halls. Why make life harder for myself?

Eventually, though, it got to a point when I finally had to tell the school, but nothing really happened. The kind of bullying I received was a subtle, mental torture over an extended period of time. It had just as devasting an impact on me as if I was physically beaten up every day of the school year.

The school's answer to my woes was to give me a learning mentor, a positively pointless individual who pretended to care. They were there simply to make me feel like I was the one who had done something wrong. I was taken out of my lessons once a week to discuss all manner of inane things, like my family and hobbies, for reasons I'm still trying to understand. Is now the right time to mention that the learning mentor's daughter was coincidentally a bully?

I went into that school as one person and came out another. Through careful mental bullying over a six-year period, all my self-belief and confidence slowly ebbed away. It left me with overwhelming insecurity and a lack of self-worth.

I saw myself in the mirror as someone else entirely. I created a new persona for those who didn't know me; I was louder, more clownish, because I'd been made to feel that way through school. When you are treated like someone else for such a long time, you become that person they tried so hard to make you. I let men choose me and went along with it as I didn't have any confidence in myself to do otherwise. The men I truly liked could stand right next to me declaring their undying love, and I wouldn't do anything about it through fear – thinking maybe they had an ulterior motive, perhaps doing it for a prank, a bet. My very small but perfectly formed family definitely noticed a change in me. At home I was more withdrawn, going from a happy child to a very unhappy teen. My mum tried her best to help but like I said before, I was too scared to do anything about it, so for many years I suffered in silence. True friends I'd made from the time before secondary school were my salvation and I think I pretended that everything was okay in front of them in a bid to retain a piece of the old me, before things changed. They may have noticed a difference but they never told me as much.

I didn't understand it at the time, but when trichotillomania and dermatillomania came into my life, they gave me some much-needed control. Suddenly, I had something through which I could channel all my pain. It was a terrible distraction.

I think if I had truly understood *why* I did it back then – if I was equipped with this 30-year-old brain filled with the knowledge and experiences I have now – I would have been better able to cope and find a way out of the darkness and into the light. Having said that, it's very easy to see things clearly *after* something has happened, because you forget how you were feeling at the time and what led you to do something in the first place. Humans are complex and irrational, and we've got to accept that sometimes there will be moments in life that don't make any sense.

Who knows whether my disorders would have ever really appeared if I was happy back then, but in my heart of hearts, I know they would have found another way to make my acquaintance.

CHAPTER 3

IT'S TIME

For a very long time I kept my disorders a secret and suffered in silence. I was too embarrassed and scared of people's reactions. When I started a recovery diary, I had just turned 29 and I was coming to the end of a very strange decade. My twenties were characterised by missed opportunities, bad decisions and illness, which you will get to know all about within these pages. At the time these things all felt very negative but now, looking back, I realise that these experiences became tools to help me face my compulsions head on. As a result, everything I've gone through has turned out to be incredibly positive.

You are probably wondering why it took me so long to get to the point where I was serious enough about stopping for good. It's very hard to understand unless you know what's happened to me in the past. It's also hard to understand if you don't know the inner workings of my brain, so I will try my best to shed some light on this.

Shaped from years of bullying at secondary school, I spent my early adult life being too scared to go for the things I truly wanted. I had next to no self-belief and gave everything up quickly without really trying, through a fear of failure and rejection. And then things changed when something altered the course of my life forever.

Five years ago, I was able to free myself from a terrible monster that had kept me prisoner and hurt me for well over 10 years. I stopped using all topical steroids and immunosuppressants, which I'd been using to treat my eczema. I made that decision because I had to; the drugs were powerful, dangerous, and came with terrible side effects like skin thinning (to the point you could clearly see my veins) and photosensitivity. The drugs gave me "perfect" skin, but it came at a price. Every time I stopped using them, my eczema – from which I had suffered since I was a baby – would come straight back, but much worse than ever before. I had spent years trying to understand why this was happening. As it turned out, it was the drugs I was given to treat my eczema that were the problem all along. They had left me with a condition far more terrible than anything that came before it. I now had red skin syndrome (RSS), a condition born from my addiction to topical steroids.

I cannot describe the fear and worry my dependency caused me over the years. I knew that using these drugs every day since becoming a teenager was a ticking time bomb, but I felt trapped, like I had no choice. I was an addict, craving the drugs that were both helping me to function like a normal person and destroying me, inside and out. I would go to the doctor's only to be told that I had "incurable" eczema and needed something stronger and more potent. This perpetuated the lie until there were no more drugs to mask what was really going on? Then what would I do?

I knew I had to do something, but in the years leading up to my eventual withdrawal, I was clueless.

Now, the answer seems so obvious that I can't believe I didn't figure it out years ago. At some point unknown to me, I had grown out of my original eczema. I didn't realise this for a long time because I now had this other condition, RSS, which mimicked the symptoms but made them ten times worse. I knew it was red skin syndrome and not eczema, because it got to a point where nothing was making sense any more. Among other clues, I noticed that many years ago – when my skin wasn't dependent on topical steroids – my eczema would clear up in the warmer months. But when my steroid-addicted skin went in the sun, I broke out in strange rashes and hives. Things weren't adding up, but when you are told you have a particular condition by those you are meant to trust, you don't question it. You just keep applying the creams you think are meant to be helping you.

That is why I couldn't understand what was happening to me for so long. But in the end, I discovered after a desperate search on Google that the only way to get better was to simply stop using topical steroids.

That "simple" answer ended up being anything but easy, and I went through things I didn't know my body was capable of. My skin oozed for months on end, I shed like a snake multiple times a day, I barely slept, and the irritation was unlike anything I had experienced in my life – as if I had itching powder all over me and was trapped within a perpetual storm of it. I was swollen like a big red balloon, and my skin constantly burned as if someone had poured acid on me. That is only a small part of what I went through during withdrawal, and I've not even covered the mental symptoms, which ranged from severe anxiety to panic attacks.

It is one thing to read about what happened, and another thing entirely to experience it for yourself. My symptoms were so severe that at times they left me housebound, but I knew I had no choice. For years I had tried everything, and I believed with all my heart that withdrawing from topical steroids was what I had to do.

To this day, it's the best and hardest decision I have ever made. I had two years of my life taken away from me as I tried desperately to reclaim my skin from the clutches of topical steroids. But sometimes it's the battles that are the hardest fought which inevitably lead to the greatest triumphs. After 26 months of hell, I came out of the process (called topical steroid withdrawal) with the best skin of my life and a newfound appreciation of everything. It was extraordinary.

Two years in which I completely changed my life, both in body and mind.

During withdrawal, I was given the rare opportunity to take a step back at a time when most people my age were rushing forwards. I did a lot of thinking about my life and the choices I had made. I finally began to understand *why* I had done things a certain way for so long. For those reasons alone, I would go through withdrawal again in a heartbeat.

My decision to write a diary about trichotillomania and dermatillomania didn't come as the direct result of some dramatic burst of resolve. This time it was more of a subtle shift in my mind. Something had changed, and I was ready both mentally and physically to do it. I had learnt enough over a very strange decade – and after literally years of torment – to know that I was equipped to deal with whatever my compulsions would throw at me.

Writing a diary wasn't a conscious decision at first. It was originally going to be an impersonal account in order for me to document how I got on. I thought I'd scrap it within hours, but very quickly – as the days passed and my determination increased – it turned into something so much more. It became a friend that I ended up pouring my heart and soul into. I told the empty pages things I had never told anyone in my life, as memories rose to the surface like a dreaded hair waiting to be plucked or a spot begging to squeezed. I suppose it was a natural progression, writing my thoughts and feelings down as I tried my damnedest to stop. Through illness, I used writing as a way of escaping from my present. It was a cathartic purge, and this period of my life was no different. Over the last five years, writing has become such a huge part of my life and to think that this diary is now a book is a little overwhelming.

When I started the diary, it was obviously with the goal to stop picking and pulling completely, but the road was far from smooth and certainly not without its problems. The end result was not how I imagined it would be. For want of a better word,

I do hope you "enjoy" my little diary. It's honest and probably quite shocking, but what I want more than anything is to give you something tangible you can hold onto: the chance of freedom ...

CHAPTER 4

TRICH DIARY

Friday 7th October 2016, 6.24pm

Okay, deep breaths. I'm going to do this.

I have a secret. When you look at me, you see clear skin. That is what I have chosen for you to see. But if you peeled away the layers, you'd find something else entirely.

I suffer from trichotillomania, or trich for short. Trich has a destructive friend called dermatillomania (derma), and together they have done everything in their power to control my life for well over 16 years.

I suppose I should tell you what these conditions actually are, but even typing their names is making me feel uncomfortable. You see, they are not something you freely share with other people. They prefer to hide in the shadows, waiting until you are on your own and at your most vulnerable before they attack. They are a shared secret between you and your mind.

Trichotillomania is a hair-pulling disorder. I have suffered with it for at least 16 years, along with dermatillomania, a skin-picking disorder. Lucky me.

They are, first and foremost, mental disorders which manifest themselves physically. On the surface, the answer to breaking free appears to be startlingly obvious: just stop touching your hair and skin! Sorted. But this is what I hate about these conditions the most. They leave you feeling weak – like a failure – because you're unable to fight the urge. They can be overwhelming in their control over you.

I hate that trich and derma are a part of who I am. I don't want them; I never have. I long to cut them out of my life.

The line between where one disorder starts and the other ends has blurred over time. And so, I feel that by putting all my energy into eradicating the beast that is trichotillomania – the compulsion I developed first – the dermatillomania will, by proxy, leave my life too.

Today has to be the day that I stop. I just can't do this to myself any more. In the last month alone, I have made approximately 8,000 statements of this nature. But every time, I end up picking and pulling at my skin within the hour. Each time it is a failed attempt.

In the past I've written break-up letters to trich. "You don't own me," I said to it. I've also destroyed many pairs of tweezers by mercilessly bending their two legs until they break apart, then chucking them in the bin with as much force as possible. None of it ever worked, though. I'd just buy more tweezers and rip up the letters filled with empty promises.

I'm not too sure why, exactly, but something about today feels different. It's like I've had a moment of clarity, as if I know *this* is the right time to finally let it go. Maybe it's because, deep down, I know that this is my last chance before it's too late for my skin to repair itself. Too late for the scars to fade.

In my heart, I know I have been gearing up to this moment for a while now and at 2.24pm, I decided I was just going to stop. It's been a little over four hours, and I haven't even felt the need to touch my skin, let alone pick at it. But I have the whole evening ahead of me, and I can only hope that the overwhelming impulse doesn't take over and make me do something I'll regret.

This morning I shaved under my arms and legs with an electric shaver and went a little crazy with my tweezers, so there is nothing at the back of my mind that will niggle at me. Hopefully that will give me the illusion of a fresh start. There is nothing like the feeling of a blank canvas – the knowledge that for one blissful moment, there is nothing to pull out or pick at. There is then the hope that maybe this time you can use that canvas to create something wonderful.

It is hard to explain to anyone who doesn't have to live with these particular compulsions what it actually feels like to know there is something on your body that you need to get out. That hair or irregular lump or bump on your skin is constantly at the back of your mind. You could be engrossed in the most incredible book or watching an epic film, but the only story you want to follow is the outcome of that hair. You become your own protagonist.

Will she get it out?

The story inevitably has a happy (or bad, depending on how you look at it) ending with the evil hair or spot banished from the kingdom of my skin.

At the moment I have a dependency as powerful as my addiction to topical steroids, or worse. I know that I cannot live my life until the thing in question – a hair, a blemish – is gone from it. When there are no hairs, there is no problem. Until they start to grow back.

Trich came into my life at a time when I was deeply unhappy. It was smart and found a way to creep up on me so gradually that I didn't realise it was there until it was too late. From then on, we were joined at the hip. We have gone through very, very bad times and some better times. I'm better now than I have been before, but I'm not quite ready yet to elaborate on what my worst was. I definitely don't think I'm ready to write about all the things I've done to my skin over the years. Maybe that will come in time, but for now my only real hope in writing all of this down is that I stand more of a chance of winning. I want it to go away.

I'm so completely and utterly bored of this condition. I am sad about all the time I have wasted, and I'm fed up of being ruled by something that should be within my power to control.

Shoulda, woulda, coulda.

In the last few months I have been gradually changing small areas of my life for the better, after years of attempting to do everything at once and getting nowhere. I have ended up making stupid decisions and going back to square one, then feeling like a total failure. Panicking has always had that effect on me. As more time passed by, it left me feeling like I hadn't achieved anything that I wanted to in life or reached the goals that had been at the top of my list for so long. And so, in haste, I have inevitably done things quickly and without much thought, trying desperately to make up for lost time, then doing the wrong thing.

Now, I look back with hindsight and see what could have been, if only I'd taken the time to do things properly. But I didn't, and here I am.

Humans are flawed, and we will all inevitably make many mistakes in life, but we have the ability to learn from them. So, this time, I'm trying to do things differently, taking more time with what I do, in order to save time in the long run. By doing that, I am actually progressing.

One bridge I still need to cross is guarded by a troll called Trich who is blocking my path. But I know that, when I cross it, it will lead the way to a wonderful life.

The areas that trich just can't leave alone right now are my legs, breasts and stomach. But if a hair were to grow on my eyebrows, bikini line or any other random spot on my body, trich would torment me until I get rid of the hair using any implement available. My favourite is naturally a pair of tweezers, but over the years I've had to get creative.

In 16 years I have never had a healthy relationship with my hair. I would like that to change. I'd like to be just a woman who simply removes excess hair from her face and body to feel pretty, and not because her very life depends on it.

Hopefully I'll write more tomorrow and document my success at not picking or pulling my skin for a whole day. But I'm scared this'll be yet another failed attempt to quit. I'm scared this Word document will go into my laptop's recycle bin, and the tweezers will appear in my hand as I make one more bid for freedom.

But I want to believe that this time I can do it. I think I can – no, I've *got* to.

Saturday 8th October 2016, 6.24pm

I write this wearing a pair of cotton gloves. I'm wearing them so that I can't feel any hairs growing through the skin on my face right at this moment – but I've got to say, they are a little redundant. I haven't even touched my skin once since I vowed to change things yesterday. Really.

Admittedly, I have been out for most of the day with my mum, and it's hard to find a moment to covertly poke and prod at your face in a busy shopping centre. Maybe I should just be with people at all times, because this has always been my little secret. That way, I might actually stand a chance of kicking this habit once and for all.

Last night went well too; I think I was riding high on the wondrous thought that this time I am going to change things for good. I'm still on that high, to be honest. I would love to find a way of keeping this momentum up. Maybe this diary is helping too. Who knows?

If I'm being honest, I am worried about tonight. I find that when I am not as busy in the evening, the night looms ahead. And before I know it, I've got one of my legs resting on the other as I scan for any elusive stray hairs; ten minutes later I'm looking more like a red, spotty leopard.

I'm going to stay positive that I can get through tonight and the earlier part of tomorrow, before I write my next entry. If I can get through tonight, I think I've got a real chance of actually beating this. I haven't lasted this long in years – but I *will* do it because I have to.

I want a life, a future, a way past the troll that blocks my path.

Sunday 9th October 2016, 6.05pm

I wanted to write this post at exactly 6.24pm, but then I realised by doing that, I'm still being controlled by something. And my end goal is to lead a free life – not bound by anything. That includes time.

I have spent too many years being controlled in one way or another – whether it be at the hands of steroid creams or the inability to stop picking or pulling at my skin. Perhaps freedom is an illusion and no one in this world is ever truly free. Most of us are trapped by something mentally or physically, but I'd like to at least give this a try.

I feel trapped by trichotillomania. It feels like a constant pull, one so powerful that it feels physical.

Shaking off my need for topical steroids gave me a glimpse of what freedom feels like. I remember times when I'd just stand still, my face pointing up to the sun, just because I could. I wouldn't feel any pain. Instead of an acid-like burning, there would be only a tender warmth. But then I would turn around to find trich and derma close behind me, keeping watch.

Last night I kept my cotton gloves on and sat next to Mum all evening. I'd asked her to keep an eagle eye on me, and as a result, I didn't touch my skin at all. This morning, though, I had about one million near misses. The only way I was able to resist was by holding my hands in makeshift claws and saying, out loud to myself, 'No, no, no. Please don't do it,' over and over again. Somehow, I was able to stay strong.

I even challenged myself to have a bath. In the past I would spend anywhere up to an hour soaking and come out looking like a pale prune. The sides of the white bath would so often be covered in short, dark hairs that I'd managed to pick out with my fingernails (or tweezers that I had smuggled into the bathroom). This time that didn't happen, although admittedly I did have a few moments where my gaze slid casually down to the hairs on my breasts, those that I have grown out like they are some kind of potted plant. I have been trying desperately to reduce the chance of them becoming ingrown again, because ingrown hairs are my weakness Instead of pulling them out, though, I just acknowledged their presence and got out of the bath, unscathed.

In the early afternoon I frantically started trying to feel the skin on my face through my cotton gloves. They kept catching on something in between my eyebrows. Straight away there was a dull tension in my whole body. I knew there was a hair there, but I was aware that I couldn't do anything about it. I felt trapped.

I spent the rest of the afternoon trying to keep myself occupied, but it was hard. At one point I realised I was sitting on my hands, rocking back and forth, in an attempt to control the rising panic. I had to do something about the hair. It was taunting me.

I have always wished for a way to physically stop myself from being able to touch my skin. I have even fantasised in the past – let's be real, I still do – about being put in a coma for a month. When I wake up, I am completely covered in hair that I can just shave off with a proper razor and shaving foam. Underneath it all is just flawless, pale skin.

It would mean I could start over. A fresh start. My blank canvas.

I have also played with the idea of being tied up or put in a straitjacket for a while. My reasoning behind that stellar thought is that if I was tied up or bound, I wouldn't be able to touch my skin, would I?

What have I become?

When it got to late afternoon, the gloves kept magically "falling off" and my hands became glued to my face. After some expert touching, I confirmed that there was indeed a thick, sharp hair growing with abandon in between my eyebrows. I also had a few lumps around the lower half of my face. At that point I knew that, if I let them, things could easily spiral out of control. So, instead, I took a deep breath and put my gloves back on, even though it felt as if they were repelling my hands like the negative ends of two magnets.

I couldn't eat with my gloves on, so at dinner time my face was once more vulnerable to attack. My hands took that opportunity and just went to town. I felt that bloody hair in between my eyebrows. I then moved on to the next stage: investigation. I rested my pocket mirror on the windowsill and saw that the hair was exactly how I feared: sharp and thick.

I swiftly moved on to the spots on my face. Because I couldn't bear the thought of them being there any longer, I squeezed them without mercy. If I'd just left it there, it would have been okay. But I then scanned my face, desperate to find something else to squeeze. I picked two lumps for the sake of it.

When I had made the lower half of my face look like the coat of a red-and-white Dalmatian, I stood back to look at what I had done. The picture in my reflection was clear: I had damaged myself. I was disgusted at how easy it was for me to go back to that dangerous mental place.

I find it fascinating how quickly things can escalate. Within moments I can go from clear-skinned to red and blotchy. I don't think I could ever adequately put into words the shame I feel, knowing that this is something I could technically – physically at least – stop myself from doing.

I know exactly what will happen and how I will feel if I continue. Yet it is as if those thoughts are eradicated by a total sense of desperation. I forget that there will ever be a tomorrow. For one blissful moment, there is only you and that hair.

But then, of course, tomorrow comes, and I have to come face-to-face with what I've done to myself. I can safely say that I have never experienced disappointment quite like that which I feel when I've picked at my skin or pulled out my hair.

I hope that one day I never have to experience it again.

This time, somehow, I was able to move away from the windowsill, close my pocket mirror and put my gloves firmly back on.

I've just looked at the clock: it's 6.24pm. Normally, something like squeezing those spots would ruin my whole day. At this stage I'd just be going on a trich and derma spree before attempting to stop again properly the next morning. It's always bloody tomorrow. That attitude is how I have dealt with everything in my life until recently, when I realised that no matter how obvious it seems, there *is* only now. That much is certain.

When I actually take a moment to think about the damage I've done today, I realise that I've made progress. I can't possibly have expected – from day one of writing a diary – a magical resolution. I couldn't have expected to never want to touch my skin again. That is absurd. This is real life, and I'm not a machine.

Instead of berating myself, I'm going to pat myself on the back and say, 'Well done.' I know from experience that it could have been so much worse.

And the blasted hair in between my eyebrows lives to see another day.

I have done a lot of thinking about why I am even bothering to write all this down. I think that, at first, it was just another attempt from a desperate woman with a deep-rooted hope (*good choice of phrase there, Cara*) that I was going to quit this time. I think part of me wanted a miraculous recovery, just because I'd written it down.

But now, I'd just like actual proof that I was able to do it. Now that I've recovered from my addiction to topical steroids, I'm gutted that I didn't write down how I felt day-to-day. It already feels like that whole dark period of my life happened to someone else. It thrills me to think that, if I take back control from my trich for good, I'll be able to read about how I was able to do it. It would be incredible to look back to when I changed such a huge part of who I am.

And, to be perfectly honest, I am finding the writing process so cathartic. When I'm brave enough to write about what I have done to my skin over the years – and the associated memories that have been rattling around in my head for so long – I hope it will make it easier to come to terms with it all. I hope I will finally be able to move on. I really don't want to have these horrible memories stuck in my head any longer. I want them gone from my life.

I *want* a life.

I don't have a plan for how long I'm going to do this, or what I'll do with it when it's finished. But ideally, I want to write every day, even if it's only a couple of words that say I'm one day closer to beating this. No matter what, I think one thing is for certain: I'm not going to stop writing until I can get to a place where trich and derma are not controlling my life. I want to get to the point where I haven't got a single scab on my skin.

I don't mind the scars I'll probably be left with, but I don't want wounds. I want a beauty routine, for God's sake, where I can shave my skin with a razor and pull my eyebrows out calmly.

Oh my goodness, the thought of a shaving routine has been a dream of mine for so long. In the past, I've tried putting plasters over any open wounds and scabs on my legs, but it's never worked. Now, this dream of mine is looking more than ever like a reality. I've got to believe that I can beat this horrible condition, otherwise what's the point? I can't let this habit stop me from living any more. I just can't.

With all that being said, I'll probably be writing in this diary until I'm an old lady. So be it.

Monday 10th October 2016, 5.59pm

It has come to my attention that a thick, sharp hair above my upper lip has joined the thick, sharp hair in between my eyebrows. There are actually two of them growing, and they have been on my mind for most of the day. I've been focusing on them so much that it's almost as if the skin around them is painful. I can practically *feel* them on my face – just the two of them – even though there are probably thousands of hairs there, stabbing at my skin.

I can hear the hairs chanting, 'Let me out! Let me out.' I am imagining scenarios and ways in which I'd pull them out – what implements I'd use, how I'd angle the tweezers or bring my fingernails together. What kind of pain would I feel if they were to come out? Would they come out easily or need a bit of a tug? I personally like to pull gently at first, to get an idea of how easy it will be before going in for the kill.

These thoughts are beautiful to me. Not knowing what it will feel like – to pull out a hair – is like the anticipation just before you're about to have a big, delicious-looking meal. In the same way that you know you will eat too much, I know that I will do some damage. But when eating, you don't think, *I'm going to be sick after this and never want to eat again.* Instead, you go into it like you've never eaten anything in your life.

I do acknowledge that even though it feels like those hairs define me entirely, I look pretty good. I am about 80 per cent better than I ever was at my worst, but I'm still not ready even to type about how bad I used to be. I will try to soon.

Now, all that remains is a small collection of scars and scabs on my legs, torso, breasts and face. Some of those areas are nearly healed, and my breasts are looking better than they have done in a long time. On my breasts and torso, I have been trying to grow out the ingrown hairs that I normally pick out as though I'm trowelling. Usually, I would see a raised red lump – the tell-tale sign of an ingrown hair – and, after a few minutes of internal battle, I'd give up and gouge the hair out from under my skin. This would leave in its wake some kind of bomb site, a crater where the follicle once was.

I may look like I am better now, but that doesn't mean trich isn't still a big part of my life. It is. Trich and derma have always been more than just scabs and scars and hair loss – they are a mindset, an attitude, a way of life that can limit what you can and can't do.

I want a healthy mind just as much as I want healthy-looking skin, and the only way to get that is to get these mental disorders out of my life.

All in all, it has been a good day. I *have* touched my face quite a bit, but as of yet that's all I've done. From about one o'clock this afternoon I kept checking the time until it was twenty-four minutes past two. That was when it was three whole days since I decided to get trich and derma out of my life. I think I need to say it once more: I haven't used tweezers in three days. That is remarkable. I can't remember a time when I haven't used them in that long.

In three days all I have done is squeeze and touch my face a little more than is healthy. There have been moments when my nails have come together like a makeshift pair of tweezers in order to get rid of those two thick, sharp hairs that are on my mind. But they are still there. Admittedly, they are taunting me with their mere presence, but this time it's more like a faint background noise rather than an omnipresent force in my head.

Can I actually do this after more than 16 years? It's been on every New Year's resolutions list for as long as I can remember. It's been the top bullet point on every body-overhaul plan I've ever had. If I can get through three picking / pulling-free days just nine more times, then that is essentially a month. A month free from picking is unthinkable, but now I want it so badly.

Please, Cara. This time you've got to do it.

Tuesday 11ᵗʰ October 2016, 6.35pm

Somehow, I have made it to just over four days without pulling a single hair out – and that bloody hair in between my eyebrows, plus its plethora of new friends, remains intact. In my entire life with trich, I don't think I've ever gone that long. That is not to say the last 24 hours have been easy – quite the opposite in fact. And today has definitely been the hardest day by far.

For the first few hours after my post last night I was great; I kept my gloves firmly *on*. My determination was fierce, but just before bed – and I don't know what made me do it – I *innocently* decided to look at my boobs. Of course, there is nothing innocent about anything to do with trich. Instantly, I located two tiny, dark hair follicles, and I was about to pick them. But before I could break the skin, I turned my hands back into makeshift claws to stop myself and I slept off the impulse.

I took another bath this morning and a spot caught my attention on my leg. It was only small. *I might as well get it*, I thought. *It's only on the surface*. And that's what I did ... but I wasn't prepared for the hair I could feel trapped underneath it. It was under the thinnest gauze of skin, and it would have been so easy to get out ... But instead, I somehow found the willpower to put my leg back under the water and attempted to relax back into the bath.

For the last few weeks I've been getting a lot of small spots on my legs – some with little hairs trapped underneath them, some with nothing. There are too many to count, and in the past I've picked at them until there were red marks on my skin. But I've found that if I don't touch them, they go away on their own.

My derma's been getting restless, though, and I've been picking. But there is no damage, so I'm not going to beat myself up about it. I'm doing my best.

I now have countless thick and sharp hairs all over my eyebrows and upper lip that I can't stop thinking about, so today's been extremely tough. I developed a pattern where I would feel them all growing, and then mould my fingers into the shape of tweezers, but before I could actually pull anything out, I would stop myself. And repeat.

In the last few hours before I reached a full four days, I was a little desperate to hit my goal. But I did question whether I could actually do it. Somehow, I made it, and that accomplishment felt amazing, but I know I need to tighten up a few habits and be stricter with myself to stand a chance of continued success. The second this entry is done, I'm going to keep my gloves on. I know they help me more than anything else.

Here's to five days free from trich. I have obviously had a few hiccups along the way, but I can deal with them. I'm a day closer to getting there.

Wednesday 12th October 2016, 6.15pm

I have made it to five days without pulling out a single hair.

I can't tell you how strange it feels to look in a mirror and see actual hairs growing. Oddly, I find that the impulse to take them out has gone. I think my main triggers now are seeing ingrown hairs or feeling the sharp ends of hairs under my fingertips. They drive me absolutely nuts. And yet, I think that the impulse to feel the hairs might be dying too. I hope so, anyway.

This morning I think I made real progress. I looked in the mirror and saw a small spot on my nose and thought to myself, *should I get it?* I really didn't want to, so I walked away from the mirror and left it alone. I'm not going to lie: there was an odd sort of pull in my chest as I put some space between me and the mirror. It was almost as if I'd left part of my soul there. There was a burning sense of unease as I stepped away from everything I know.

I don't know who I am if I walk away – that is not what I do! I like the comfort, the blissful anticipation I get when I know exactly what's going to happen next. But I never feel blissful afterwards, of course.

The spot on my nose is still there, along with that now lengthy hair in between my eyebrows and a moustache most men would kill for – come next week, I won't even recognise myself.

Even getting to five days since I last pulled a hair out is something that always felt out of my reach. To actually achieve this is mind-blowing. If I can reach a week, I know I can do anything I put my mind to.

First, the tweezers, then the world.

I've just looked at the time. It's 6.24pm; I'll take it as a sign that someone out there agrees with me.

Thursday 13th October 2016, 7.40pm

Day six: *Completed!* I can't believe I actually just wrote those words. Jesus. I feel like I could actually start braiding with the hair in between my bloody eyebrows, it's getting so long now.

Last night passed in a lovely blur – I had no issues. But early this morning something stressful happened. An unreasonable eBay buyer demanded their money back for something I had sold, even though I knew I'd been completely honest in the ad. Within moments, I wanted to return to the familiar. I wanted to feel my comfort blanket all around me, to be able to cocoon myself within the knowledge that I could take away some of the overwhelming pressure on myself.

I instantly found myself attached to my skin, feeling all the new stubbly hairs and bringing my fingernails together like a vice, ready to pull them out at any moment. I ran up to the bathroom and my eyes immediately scanned my bikini line, searching desperately for something to take my mind off the cause of the stress. I longed to feel the prickle of hairs against my fingertips, the stretching of my skin, the sensation of hairs leaving their tight follicles.

It probably sounds a little crazy that something regarded as painful is a comfort to some people, but it is. I have heard in the past that those who cut themselves say it is like a release. A quick search on Google tells me that it's something to do with all the endorphins running around your body when you hurt yourself. I have always thought of my particular issues with trich and derma to be more like self-harm than anything else. I experience actual moments of euphoria when a hair comes out or a spot disperses just as I hoped it would. The desire to harm myself is like a tingle. My fingertips twitch at the thought.

It's a desire that can so easily be fulfilled.

Today, I did all that touching, but I didn't end up doing any damage. Every single hair survived my ordeal. I don't know if that's because my desire to pick is weakening as each day passes sans tweezer intervention. Perhaps my desire and desperation to stop is simply increasing, or maybe it's just plain old luck – who knows?

Regardless, it's a victory that I'll gladly take.

Like many people, stress affects me badly, and I'm still working on that. Last year, I started using meditation for my skin condition, and I found the effects quite extraordinary. But since then, my concentration has slipped, making it impossible to clear my mind enough to do it. I am going to try to get back into it to see if it can help me with my trich banishment.

I am still not wearing my gloves much, but I'm wondering whether it's better I keep them off, as I don't really want to live my life looking like I'm perpetually about to break into mime. And if I *did* decide to leave them on, would it just be harder when they eventually came off? I think I'll keep them on as much as possible for the next few days, then wear them a little less from Monday. For the last few weeks, I've been working from home after moving back in with my mum and I suppose I have had more time to let trich invade my life. But I think I've done okay.

Tomorrow marks a week since I started this journey (a whole week – what?!) and I think it's safe to say that I'm excited about it. I'm going to be confident and say now that no matter what, I'm going to reach that milestone. Absolutely *nothing* is going to stop me.

Friday 14th October 2016, 6.50pm

One. Week.

It was touch and go for a second there, and literally moments before starting this post, I felt myself beginning to cave. But I saved myself at the last minute, put my pyjama trouser down and began typing instead.

Since I started this new adventure, I have been putting Sellotape around the bottom of any loose-legged trousers I wear so I don't have easy access to my legs. It must be working, as the only time I've slipped is when I didn't do the Sellotape trick.

Last night involved lots of touching and feeling – the usual really – but I think I was so engrossed in the final episode of *Breaking Bad* season four that I didn't have a chance to pick.

In the bath this morning – as I am apparently a bath woman now – I found myself examining ingrown hairs again, the type of which I call a "trich-tease". Feeling frustrated despite my newly acquired willpower, I took a deep breath and put my leg back into the now tepid bath. I knew I was only hours away from reaching a milestone in my amazing new journey.

What makes it harder to leave ingrown hairs like that is the fact that I just *know* they would be so easy to get out, although sometimes that's deceptive and I can end up leaving behind a real mess.

It's great now that the weather is colder, as it's the season of black tights and trousers. I can hide my now-hairy legs under thick fabric. Before, it was the season when I could easily hide my red, scabby legs. Maxi-dresses were also a godsend. Pre-trich, I loved swimming, but I can count on one hand the times I dared to get into a pool during the calmer phases of my trichotillomania.

Summer has always been tricky. Whenever the weather occasionally got hot enough that only a skirt, shorts or dress would suffice, I'd have to wear concealer and nude fishnet tights. They would hide the evidence of my battle with a mental disorder that was slowly destroying me.

In the last week, I have found that all my fingernails have started growing. I suppose using them as makeshift tweezers for so long can wear them down. The thumbnail on my left hand, after years of being so weak, is actually starting to recover.

The gloves are staying on until I can be trusted to not touch myself. I sound like a horny 14-year-old boy.

At this moment, I couldn't be more grateful that a week ago I started this challenge. Here's to many more trich-free weeks.

CHAPTER 5

THE SWIMMING PARTY

I loved swimming when I was younger. I would compete in galas at school and go swimming for fun. I'd go to swimming parties or even swim by myself, just to be in the water. But when trich came into my life, slowly but surely swimming became a thing of my past.

There is nothing like the feeling of cool water flowing past your skin; you feel so alive as you glide through the water. But after I developed trich, all I'd feel as I went into the water was the stone-cold fear of infection, the worry that I'd have people staring at me in judgement. I was terrified that people would be disgusted at the wounds on my body, as if I was diseased.

Even if you have only one blemish or flaw on your body, you could still feel that self-conscious. These marks take you far beyond the physical. Trichotillomania and dermatillomania are mental disorders, and that one mark can have just as much power over you as a body covered in lesions.

Where you see a scab, I see isolation and despair.

One time, someone brought up the idea of going to an outdoor water park to celebrate a birthday that I had already promised I would go to. I can still feel the jolt of panic that shot up my spine at the thought of it. It was a time when my trich and derma were particularly bad, and there would be no hiding it. My secret would be out there in the open for all to see. I suppose I could have shown up in some kind of full-body wetsuit – but why the hell would I?

I cannot begin to describe my relief when the idea for the water park was scrapped – my secret was safe.

For many years I've told myself that once I stop picking and pulling at my skin, I'll swim again. I even have this beautiful swimming costume waiting patiently in my drawer: a black and bronze high leg. It's *uber*-flattering, with a zip running all the way up to the neck …

For a long time it has remained folded – hidden away, but never forgotten.

Saturday 15th October 2016, 5.40pm

Straight after finishing my diary entry last night, and because I'd been reminded I had ingrown hairs, I rather ironically decided to look at the damn things. Mistake. You may be confused as to why a random, hard hair (gulp) could send me into raptures. So, let me try to enlighten you. I want you to imagine someone you are very attracted to walking into the room you're in. Maybe you like tall men (guilty); maybe you like 'em dark and hairy (guilty, again); maybe you have a thing about nice arms (er …).

There is an emotion, or perhaps a feeling, which can affect your entire being, an inexplicable force making you want to be near this person. That is how I feel with my trich and derma: I can take or leave a large proportion of the hairs on my face and body (and the hair on my head is like another species entirely), but if a hair or spot has certain attributes, I will not wait. In the same way that some people don't want to wait for a second date to take their crush home with them, I want it *now*.

Humans are strange.

Sunday 16th October 2016, 6.35pm

I got into quite a panicky / anxious place last night. It all started, like it always does, as a small, harmless thing: I touched a hair, the consistency of a piece of elastic, that has been growing for the last few days directly underneath the dratted hair in between my eyebrows. For some reason I started freaking out that it had gone, and there began half an hour where I obsessively tapped and bounced every single sharp, thick hair on my whole face, just to make sure they were all there. I just couldn't seem to get it into my head whether the hairs were there or not – it was like my mind was not sending confirmation to the right part of my brain. I stopped myself from doing it after a while, but it wasn't easy and there was no closure. There was just a dull ache in my stomach. I am still trying to understand why I got so worked up about it, but I think it must be something to do with the fact that I want to be rid of trich and derma so much it's like a deep, constant agony. I could scream at the futility of how I've felt sometimes when I've pulled something out that I didn't want to or caused a mark on my skin that I tried so hard not to create.

The fear of taking a step back now, when I have come further than I think I have in over half my life, is too painful to bear. I just can't go back – I can't feel that terrible disappointment again. I can't wait any longer for scabs to heal or hairs to grow back. I want this now, and I'm not waiting another 16 years to get over it.

After making banana bread, I spent the rest of the afternoon working on a photo collage of women with amazing skin, as a sort of goal that I can look at when I'm struggling to remember why I can't get *just one hair*. They are all topless, and even having them on my computer makes me feel a little nervous. I've even labelled the folder they are in "body inspiration", just in case anyone looks on my computer and gets the wrong idea.

Monday 17th October 2016, 6.26pm

Honestly, I have no idea what I'm talking about today as I'm starving and absolutely shattered. That's probably a good thing as I couldn't be bothered to pick or touch my skin tonight even if I wanted to. I'm going to start meditation before bed as well – if I don't fall asleep in the process. After recovering from my terrible skin condition just over a year ago, I was so utterly desperate to stay well that I implemented meditation into my life.

Going into it, I was sceptical. I didn't think that it could really have an impact on my skin. But it did and, more importantly, my mental health changed dramatically. During topical steroid withdrawal – a hellish time of my life – I experienced severe anxiety. In fact, it was so acute that I developed a temporary phobia (they call it trypophobia: a fear of holes). It also heightened all my other emotions, such as fear, doubt and worry, until I was left paralysed by it. After withdrawal, I would wake up in the middle of the night, gripped by a panic attack, terrified that my skin would flare up again and that this lovely new skin was only temporary.

Meditation dampened down the flames raging in my mind. It didn't put the fire out completely, but it was enough to change everything for me. I suppose you could say that's a pretty solid reason for wanting to try it for my trich and derma. The issue with meditation, though, is that it's a giant faff, one of those activities that is so easily pushed out of your day. You often end up saying, 'I'll do it tomorrow.' I've tried to keep it up where possible over the last year, but I've definitely slipped and got back into bad habits. Today I'd like to change that.

Tuesday 18th October 2016, 6.24pm

I use this in the literal sense and not as some kind of elaborate excuse, but last night – without meaning to – I made a hair on my leg fall out. I shall explain. The hair was the sort that falls out with only with the slightest of nudges. I was only, for want of a better word, *innocently* touching it. And before I knew it, it was gone.

I freaked out for a moment, thinking that I had spoiled everything and I'd have to start this whole journey again. But now, I think those kinds of things are sent as a sort of test to see how you will react, to see whether you'll just move on when you have a setback, no matter how big or small. So, I swallowed down the impulse to actually pull some hairs out and fail fabulously, and instead, I put on my gloves and pretended to forget about it.

This incident happened the second I took the tape off my pyjama bottoms last night, so from now on I'm going to have to keep the tape on until the moment before I close my eyes to go to sleep.

I obviously can't be trusted ... yet.

I don't think that a hair "falling out" should change anything. I started this journey on the 7th October, and while trich may have got its petty revenge last night, that doesn't mean it *has* to win. Trich knows it is losing, and it's now trying anything it can to get through to me.

But you shan't, trichotillomania. Not this time.

I also started to pick at the dry spots on my legs, so I think I need to ignore them for a few weeks and then try dry body brushing, as I have a feeling it's just because I probably need to exfoliate or something. We'll see anyway, because I'm not sure if even picking at them counts as being a dermatillomania issue. It probably is, but I know nothing any more.

I feel when I write in this journal it's impossible to lie about what I have done to my skin – as though my nose will start growing really long if I even consider leaving out a single incident. It's only a bloody Word document, and yet it feels like the strictest authoritarian in the world, one that I desperately want to please. I'm sorry – don't hate me, diary!

I suppose all of this stems from my poor, confused mind's desire for conformity. I have been striving for a perfection in my skin that I know will never come. No one is perfect, and neither is their skin. I don't like to see anything which interferes with the way I believe my skin should look, and anything irregular throws everything off balance. Strange hairs almost set off alarm bells in my mind. I can almost hear a speaker booming, 'Mayday, mayday! We have a code red situation here.' And the only way to silence the voices is to eradicate any hair that doesn't conform.

I wish there was some way of muting that deafening inner voice and just accepting who I am completely, but I can't. Yet. At least, I hope it's yet.

I'm saying this like it's some profound realisation I've just had, but I know I have just got to leave my skin *alone* for a few weeks, otherwise it defeats the entire object of this exercise. I still have a seriously unhealthy relationship with my skin, as today has clearly shown me. I am absolutely amazed at what I have been able to achieve since I decided to tackle this addiction of sorts, but I still have a long way to go.

I may not be covered in scabs any more, but derma is still very much there, and it's enough to make me feel trapped by it. The other thing I've realised I have to do is stop putting so much pressure on myself and setting such strict rules. In all areas of my life that has inevitably led to failure. Set rules *never* work for me. If I put pressure on myself to do something, I'll panic and do the polar opposite. I know what I need to do, and I've shown that it can be done. I just need to do it.

I feel like this is something to do with the fact that even though I don't want to admit it, I feel like a disappointment – not good enough. It's as though I don't deserve to be happy or have anything I truly want. I think part of me is also scared of what would happen if I actually did stop; then, I'd have nothing to fall back on, nothing on which to blame my lack of progress. I'd be in this new, unknown land without my crutch, feeling like that person at a party who doesn't know anyone there.

There is an awful part of me that wants to jeopardise everything I do for exactly those reasons, and I have no one else to blame but myself. Now, I'm so scared of doing anything wrong, because one bad move could waste so much precious time. And I don't have time to spare.

Panicking about lost time inevitably leads to more time wasted.

Wednesday 19th October 2016, 6.38pm

Keep me busy like today and I'll never have a problem with my skin again. I have literally been on my laptop working from half-past seven this morning, and I still won't be done for at least an hour. I haven't really thought about picking, let alone found the time to do it.

All I have to mention is pretty positive: this afternoon when I went to the bathroom, I found myself with my foot propped up on the opposite knee, scanning my bare leg. I started to pick at a dry spot, but instead I said – out loud to myself – 'I can't be bothered.' Progress.

Good night.

Thursday 20th October 2016, 6.53pm

The last couple of days have been so mad that I'm struggling to write more than a few lines in this diary. That's been great for tackling my problems with trich – it's been feeling unloved and restless. You don't like that, do you, trich? Not nice, is it?

Even if I wasn't very busy, I think I would have noticed some improvements. Last night the gloves stayed on, but I was so tired that I was nearly asleep taking the tape off the bottom of my pyjamas.

This morning was immensely positive too. On Tuesday I started a basic Pilates workout, one that I did again today. I find it a little more comfortable keeping my legs bare while doing Pilates, as I prefer the freedom to move without any obstructions. Well, as I lay on my yoga mat this morning and flung my legs towards myself like the instructor told me to, I came face-to-face with a dry spot on my leg. In the spirit of Pilates, I "zenned" out and pretended it didn't exist. I did think about it some more, but I haven't touched it at all.

After Pilates I went up for my shower and decided to try something: I kept the door to the bathroom open but the light switched off. That way there was enough light to see what I was doing – therefore I wouldn't do something dangerous, like slip on some soap and fall to my death – but it wasn't light enough for me to see anything on my skin. It worked out perfectly, and I survived without incident. Here's to showering in darkened rooms from now on.

In the last hour I've found myself playing with sharp hairs by hooking them under my nails. It is hard to explain how good it feels, but there is something so glorious about the dull thickness of a hair trapped underneath your nail. Oh my goodness, it is wonderful. Yes, my gloves should have been on, but on the plus side, I'm finding that I am indulging in this guilty pleasure of mine much less. I suppose that's progress, but I do wonder if I'll ever get to the point where I do that and think, *meh*. A girl can dream, can't she?

I think, in a way, I'm a little reluctant to quit doing it because it feels so good. *Pull yourself together, Cara!*

Earlier, I looked down at my body and couldn't believe it was *my* skin. It was just so beautiful. Even though I know the scars will reappear when I get in hot water or have a bit of irritation or something, today they were really pale. For a moment, I felt like a woman again.

It's hard to even admit this in a personal diary, but I haven't been with anyone for years, and I know it's mostly down to trich. Your twenties are apparently meant to be this carefree existence where you have all these *fabulous* experiences and go on lots of dates with *fabulous* men. You're supposed to have a great time, but for years I have run away from almost every opportunity that could lead to meeting a potential partner. I am so scared and worried that someone I like might discover my secret and be repelled by it. As a result, I've unwittingly stayed as celibate as a nun.

There have been times when I've pushed myself to live a little and go out on a few dates – something that happens very rarely – but even before I meet up with them for the first time, I start thinking ahead and panicking. Often, I take some deep breaths and make yet another heartfelt but flimsy vow: *Okay, Cara. You've got to stop picking now. In a couple of weeks, maybe, when you've healed, you should be okay.*

I always try my best to stop, but the added pressure to give up – on top of the existing pressure I have put myself under for years – is way too strong. I end up picking more than I did before. I suppose trich has been like the best friend a girl could ask for; it's probably steered me clear of many a dating disaster.

Thanks, Trich. Now go away.

CHAPTER 6

THE BOY

In my early twenties I had a crush on a guy. He had dirty blond hair and the kind of facial hair that made him look ever so much like a cavalier – something I have always been wildly attracted to. Up until then, I had spent my life running away from those I truly liked due to a lack of self-belief. Instead, I settled for – and was chosen by – men whom I deemed "safe".

But no matter how hard I tried to stop myself from liking this guy, I had to face the facts: I *did* like him, very much. I liked him so much that whenever he walked into the room I would get butterflies.

Want to hear something utterly terrible? I think he liked me too.

You're probably wondering why that could ever be considered a bad thing. But to me it was, because he risked tearing down the carefully constructed walls I had built around myself. Anything that upset the delicate equilibrium of my "safe" life was a threat to me. I was scared of trusting someone. I was scared that I wasn't enough. It was too much.

At this point my legs were in a very bad state. And even though I was a master at masking my "dirty little secret", dating means literally stripping away those barriers so that the other person can see who you truly are – and I couldn't do that. It would have left me vulnerable to rejection and ridicule, just for being me.

There are many reasons why I dated very little in my twenties, but trich and derma are definitely major factors in all the decisions and choices I've made. This guy in particular tried very hard to engage with me – he even flirted with me. And all I did was treat him with open hostility. Whenever we were finished talking, I'd scrunch my eyes up in embarrassment and make a vow that the next time we talked I'd do better. Somehow, I'd make him believe that I was interested.

I never did.

I do think about him from time to time. I think about what could have been if trich and derma simply weren't there. Who knows? Not pursuing it could have saved me from heartbreak. But then again, what's worse: trying and failing, or not trying at all?

I'm always wondering, *what if?*

Friday 21st October 2016, 6.02pm

Another 24 hours have passed, and now I am two weeks into my challenge. Oh. My. *God!* Last night was great, and the only thing that consumed me was season five of *Breaking Bad*. I found myself so captivated by the programme that I didn't even think about trich. That's quite an amazing accomplishment, seeing that every single night since I started this journey – no matter how tired I've been – trich has been one of the last things I have thought about before going to sleep. So, I'd like to take a moment to thank Walt, Jesse, Hank, Skyler and co. for helping me through last night.

Trich only made an appearance when I was in the bath this morning and forgot to turn off the light. So, there I was, stuck, already submerged in the water, my skin illuminated and exposed to my hungry eyes. As I scanned my legs, I saw approximately one thousand things I wanted to pull out in about five seconds flat, including a flimsy, curly black hair on my right leg that appeared to be growing from the same follicle as a regular hair (audacious bastard).

God, it would have been *so* easy to get that out.

Even though I didn't actually touch, pick or pull my skin, I made no attempt to look away. I just sat there in the warm bath, staring at my skin as my fingers pruned up.

I've been in an odd mood for most of the day. Early this morning, after putting all my energy into writing something I am very excited about, I found that I was a little deflated.

I couldn't be bothered with anything else – to-do lists, looking after myself, eating well. I couldn't bring myself to care, to be honest. But now I'm writing in this diary again – at just past six in the evening – all the excitement and passion that's been lacking since this morning is flowing back into me. This diary started off as something I thought would be over before it had a chance to really begin. I thought it would end up being another forgotten hope that would perish and get thrown into my recycle bin. But now it's nearly 10,000 words long and crammed with thoughts and memories that I never thought I'd ever write down. In the space of two weeks, it has become a big part of my life and something I have loved writing every day.

Even though I know I will feel unparalleled joy when trich finally leaves my life for good, I know I'll be sad not to write this any more. It's almost as if I'll be losing one of the most supportive friends I've ever had, whose only goal has been to look out for me and help me fight for the freedom that has been lost to me for over 16 years.

Dear Diary, I love you.

Saturday 22nd October 2016, 2.30pm

I realised something quite extraordinary today. Apart from the odd ingrown hair, I have absolutely no desire to pick or pull at the hair under my arms. It actually turns me off. I find that astounding, seeing as it all started there.

At the beginning of my nightmare with trich and derma, I was obsessed with my underarms, so much so that I would do absolutely anything to get hairs out of that area. It didn't matter where I was or what I was doing; if I knew there was a hair to get out, I'd do it. Once, when I was younger and attacking my underarms quite badly, I was at a friend's house (that friend shall respectfully remain nameless). I was happily playing along with them, but at the back of my mind the desire to pull something out was growing very strong. In the end, I pretended that I needed to go to the toilet. And then I started pulling hairs out with my fingers.

I didn't want to take a long time in the bathroom so I tried to do it quickly, but there was this one hair that I couldn't seem to get with my fingers. I remember frantically searching everywhere in this bathroom for some tweezers. I eventually found some. They were part of this blue grooming kit – but they were dirty. I hate even remembering this part, but I was so desperate to get the hair out that I didn't even bother washing them first. I just flung my arm up in the air and got to work.

I remember how the tweezers felt in my hands. They were very heavy – for men, I think – and so blunt. I had to really twist them into my skin to get them to work. But in the end, I caught the thing that had consumed me and I found some release. This release never lasted, but for that small moment it was as if I had somehow managed to achieve world peace. All was well.

Afterwards, I left the bathroom and played with my friend again like nothing had happened. My underarm was sore. Thankfully, that story does not end with me getting a serious infection.

God, I needed to get that out. I'm scared because I've never told anyone that before. And I must say, dear Diary, you are a sympathetic listener. I have decided that when trich has left my life and I finish writing here, I am going to show this to my mum. I want her to know everything. Even though I think she needs to read it all, I'm sad at the thought of it. She has been there for me in every possible way, and over the years she has tried her best to stop me from picking and pulling. But how can you possibly control someone who will not quit, no matter what?

My mum never physically restrained me from doing it, but she definitely tried everything in her power to make me stop. First, she tried the soft, gentle approach – reaching out to let me know she was there to help me. Other times, she would be strict and tell me off. 'You've got to stop now,' she'd say. 'This can't go on.' She would hide tweezers, cuticle clippers and other implements that I could use to pick or pull with, and she would stop me locking the bathroom door. When it was very bad, she would stay with me while I was in the bath and make sure I couldn't use that time to do it. She would sense when I was leaving a room to pick or pull, and follow me out.

But in the end, she gave up. I have realised recently that the only person capable of making you stop doing anything is *you*. Mum saw the wounds I couldn't hide, but there is still so much she doesn't know – until now.

So, Mum, I'm very, very sorry.

When I first got out of the bath this morning, I saw a lot of old scars all over my body that always appear when I get hot or my skin feels irritated. They fade quickly now, especially the ones on my legs, and I can only hope that means they are going for good.

What would it be like to not have many scars at all? I say not many, because I know there are some that will never fade.

But I'm fine with that; they are part of me. I am thinking more about what it will be like when I look at my skin, and trich and derma scars are not the only things I can see. I look forward to not giving them a second thought.

God, that will be wonderful.

You know, I am past hoping that I'll get through this. I have come too far now – I *will* do it.

Sunday 23rd October 2016, 6.11pm

Since my last entry, it's been interesting, to say the least. A lot has happened in my trich world; some good, some bad.

I should probably start by saying that last night trich and derma teamed up against me and had their first tiny victory. It started like it normally does: not learning from my previous mistakes, I took off the tape wrapped around the bottom of my trousers too early because I thought I could handle it. I couldn't. I took the tape off at about half-past five, so I had the entire evening ahead of me, and Trich made the most of it.

Naturally, because the tape was off my legs, I didn't bother with my gloves either. It was all innocent at first – the roll up of a trouser leg, a glance, a fleeting touch – but over the next few hours, I saw more and more things on my legs that were bothering me. My desire grew when I saw a couple of those dry spots on my legs, and then I finally caved in. I started, gently, picking some of them off. I will say that no actual damage was done, but it's the act itself that is the problem; something that looks small now can so easily turn into scars later.

I continued to pick and pull, but at about nine o'clock I actually said out loud to myself, 'Come on now, Cara. Let's not do this any more, okay?'

I actually did put my leg down. I walked back downstairs with a different attitude, determined not to let derma have its wicked way with me again.

Now, I *may* have had this lovely new attitude, but did that mean I put those gloves of mine back on? Of course not. Because I had deemed my legs out of bounds, I started feeling for all the thick hairs on my face. For about an hour before bed, I played with three exceptionally thick hairs on my upper lip. I knew without a doubt that I had got past the point where I could stand them being there any longer.

It was when I was lying in bed and trying to sleep that I decided to get the party started. There was no time for tweezers, though. I just brought my two well-trained fingernails together and pulled and pulled.

I almost moaned out loud. The relief was extraordinary. It's hard to put into words how it feels, but imagine you have been on your feet all day. You're tired and aching all over, and then there's a moment when you are finally able to lie down on the most comfortable bed in the whole world. That feeling comes close – that, or the exquisite feeling of taking your bra off at the end of a long day.

Last night, when I had pulled out the hairs that had been really bothering me, I decided I would tackle the rest in the morning. My plan was formed. I then tried to sleep, but all I could do for hours was toss and turn. Giving up on the idea of slumber for a while, I did some thinking about everything, including trich.

There was a hollow sadness in my chest at the thought of what I had just done. I had come so far, further than I ever had in 16 years. And now, in the space of a few hours, I had undone some of my hard work. At that moment my resolve returned: I didn't want to do this to myself any more.

I also knew that I just wasn't ready to use tweezers again. I would rather look like a yeti when I see my friends next Thursday than slip back into old habits and inevitably do enough damage that I'd have to start this whole journey again.

It was as if trich and derma thought I was dead on the floor and they were celebrating the fact. But when their backs were turned, I slowly got up and fought once more. I wasn't ready to admit defeat. I woke up with a renewed determination to fight trich and derma until they were only a distant memory.

In reality, I have only done a tiny bit of damage; but that does not end a journey. It started on Friday 7th October 2016, and it hasn't finished yet. I'm fighting this.

Now, I'm even more determined to do this. I know that the only way I stand a chance of winning is if I am vigilant and aware of what I am doing at *all* times. I have asked my mum to tell me constantly to wear my gloves, keep the light off in the bathroom and keep that bloody tape wrapped around the bottom of my pyjamas. Also, above the desk that I sit at pretty much all day every day, I have stuck a piece of paper on the wall that says *"GLOVES, TAPE, LIGHT."*

Those three things are my weapons. Trich and derma *may* have won this round, but I'm going to win the battle.

With renewed vigour this morning, I shaved my legs and underarms with my electric shaver, ready for seeing my friends next Thursday. I shoved my gloves on first thing and wrapped plenty of tape around the bottom of my trousers. And a few hours later when I had a shower, that blasted light stayed *off*.

This afternoon I started watching videos on YouTube about trichotillomania. It's hard to explain why, but I found it immensely hard and comforting at the same time to see actual human beings fighting the same battle as me. They understood the desperate compulsion, the *need* to do it, and it's truly made me feel not so alone.

I still need to do a little more digging, as the people I watched didn't have my exact problem. Most people seemed to only pull the hair on their head, but it still helped. I think having something like trichotillomania or dermatillomania makes you feel like you don't belong, that you are the only human in the world that has these flaws. They make you feel like everyone else is perfect and that it is just you who is weak, dirty, an embarrassment.

No one else would ever have disorders like these. Come on, just stop touching your skin if you're so unhappy about it!

I believe compulsions like trich and derma really feed on a person's desire to keep them a secret. They love our isolation. So, knowing that there are others suffering and fighting loosens some of the hold they have on you. You realise you are not the only one fighting, and having trichotillomania or dermatillomania doesn't make you weak or dirty.

You are simply you. You are perfectly imperfect, like everyone else in the world. Everyone else is battling their own demons and believing that no one else will understand.

It's thirty-four minutes past six now, and since my small relapse last night I've been really good. But the first day post slip-up is always the easiest, so I will let time be the real test of my willpower. Then again, after eating all the chocolate last night, the faith I have in my willpower has been severely tested. I think I've written enough for now – I'm shattered after next to no sleep last night, and I'm very much looking forward to testing my willpower. Jesus.

This post is dedicated to those brave hairs that didn't make it through the night. To the hair in between my eyebrows, in particular: thank you for everything. With your demise, I shall rise from the ashes and grow stronger again.

Monday 24th October 2016, 6.06pm

I have been doing a lot of thinking today about my future with this diary and my journey from this point on. I've come up with a plan and an end goal that I think will work well for me. After this week, I plan on not seeing anyone but my mum for at least a month – a whole month during which I won't pull out a single hair or pick mercilessly at any spots. In that time, I am going to leave my skin and hair completely alone.

Some might think the idea of not seeing anyone for a whole month is some kind of punishment. But even though I love the company of others, the time I get to myself is precious, and seeing as I am currently living with Mum in the heart of the English countryside, I am able to do exactly that. I suppose I would call myself a bit of an introvert, and after two years of enforced solitude through illness, I am able to adapt easily. I've always found that time away is when I'm most able to grow.

I can feel Derma having a small breakdown at the thought of a month in solitude, and Trich is already sharpening its arsenal of small knives to chip away at my willpower. In the last two weeks I've achieved things that I didn't think were possible, and I definitely know that I can do a whole month. It's terrifying in a way, but in that time my plan is to get hairier and hairier until I turn into something that Cousin Itt would be proud of. Then, at the end of that time, I will take my place on the podium and claim my victory against trich and derma.

So, let's say, then, that on Thursday 24th November 2016, exactly a month from now, I shall be closing the door on trich and derma for the last time.

I'm not saying that on that date I'll never have the compulsion to do anything bad to my skin again. I'm not saying it will be some kind of magical resolution. I just know that if I can get through a month, learn how to manage the compulsion, and get used to not touching my skin, I'll be able to handle the rest of my life. Perhaps one day trich will be just something I did in my past. I think I need to mark that date in the only way I see fitting: by taking a long, hot bath in which I shave my legs properly with shaving foam and my razor, which has been gathering dust in its packaging for months now, waiting patiently for this momentous day. I will then proceed to pluck my eyebrows and upper lip and tackle the other body hairs that have given me trouble over the years. What makes it exciting is that I will be able to do all this in a healthy way; without compulsion, without anxiety.

On the 24th November I will also be making my last diary entry. My gut tells me it's the right thing to do, as I need to move on from this and enjoy my newfound freedom. Goodness, I'm going to miss writing here. But the idea of that foamy bath is so exciting and surreal. I think if I keep this diary going any longer, I would be acknowledging that trich is still a large part of my everyday life.

And so, dear Diary, I shall make the most of our time together, then be on my way.

Tuesday 25th October 2016, 6.10pm

I have lost count of how many days into this journey I am now. That's a statement I never thought I'd make, as I don't think I truly expected to get this far when I started. I do know that on Friday it will be three weeks since I made a vow to stop picking and pulling once and for all. Of course, it goes without saying that my journey has been bumpy, but I accepted a while ago that it's about keeping going and not thinking that all blips are failures. Blips make it interesting; you learn from them. I certainly have, and I'm sure there are going to be many more blips in my future.

A few days ago, I mentioned that I had found some YouTube videos about trich. Last night I realised one of the women who suffers with it has a *whole separate channel dedicated to the subject!* After watching about four or so of her videos, I was stunned. It was like she was verbalising all the thoughts and feelings that have been inside my head for years. I'm really not alone, am I?

There were videos where she had documented her disappointment over pulling again and the total despair of it. After watching them last night, I felt completely overwhelmed and profoundly grateful. So, I did something I very rarely do: I wrote a comment on one of her videos – a public comment that anyone in the world could see if they wanted to. I made my first confession, typing the words I have been unable to write for over 16 years:

I suffer with trichotillomania.

It felt so good. No one may ever see it, and I am sure it will soon be lost among the sea of other people commenting. But it doesn't matter; it's not about that. I just had to reach out and tell her how much I value her videos. And by doing so, I confessed my deepest, darkest secret to the whole world.

Her name is Beckie Jane Brown, and she is my new best friend.

Doing this last night solidified my resolve to do something else too. As I have said many times now, on Thursday I am seeing a group of my closest friends. Somehow, I plan to very casually drop it into the conversation that I have secretly suffered with trichotillomania and dermatillomania for well over 16 years. No big deal. Then, at subsequent meetups over the next few months, I will slowly add in more details of what I have done to my skin, until they feel as if they have known about it all along.

I know I don't have to tell anyone if I don't want to, but I feel that before I can truly heal from this and move on, I need to tell everyone I know that I have these conditions. I need to make it common knowledge. It sounds easy, but the idea of it makes me feel a little sick. I feel like they will be sick when I tell them.

I mean, when I had my skin condition, I couldn't believe how supportive the people were around me. They stuck by me through it all, but this is different. To me, trich has always felt like something dirty, so for me to actually admit that I have this is like saying *I'm* dirty.

Apart from the odd time in secondary school – when I would walk into class with holes gouged out of my face that I was unable to conceal, making up excuses like, 'Damn that acne!' – no one has ever had a clue that I've even so much as touched my skin, let alone damaged it badly. No one has known apart from my mum, and I've already said that she has had to suffer through some very painful times with her daughters, Cara and Trich. Even Mum isn't aware of everything I have done to myself over the years.

I think my grandmother knew a little about it too, but only vaguely, and I don't think she understood the magnitude of the problem and how serious it was. I have a rather horrible memory of a time during school when I was particularly unhappy and really struggling with my trich. Nanny saw me picking under my arms and told my mum – all because she cared. Mum then told me, and I felt betrayed and as a result, I didn't talk to my nan for a little while after that. Now, this person I loved very dearly is gone, and I can't say I'm sorry.

Trich, I cannot tell you how good it will be when you are out of my life.

This morning I made a boo-boo and left the light on in the bathroom when I had my shower. There was a hair I'd forgotten about until that moment – one that had the nerve to grow out of a *hair follicle that was already taken*. It wanted to remind me it was still there. It's now growing at an odd angle, meaning it has turned into a hair that would come out easily. It is now the ultimate temptation, like Eve's apple. I reached for the forbidden fruit, and even had the thing loosely trapped between two fingernails when I remembered myself and how far I had come. I relaxed my grip on the hair and let the hot water wash away any temptation.

It sounds quite absurd, but I then spent the better part of the afternoon flashing myself. Every time I felt an urge, I would basically stop what I was doing and pull my bra top down – just to check on my boobs and make sure that those bloody hairs there were still alive and kicking. I repeated this approximately a thousand times within the space of a few hours. Everything lived to tell the tale – and apparently I'm a pervert now.

A couple of hours later, I pulled a few eyebrow hairs out for my mum. I can see her blonde hairs better, but she asked me first to make sure it was okay, just in case it would tempt or trigger me. I felt absolutely nothing at all – nada. I am noticing tiny changes in my response to excess hairs and the level of desire I feel towards the act itself. I am much calmer and more detached. It's definitely not this all-consuming thing like it was before.

Only time will tell exactly how much I have changed but for now, I'm happy.

Wednesday 26th October 2016, 7.27pm

I am worried about the amount of time I have spent today thinking about that bloody tease of a black hair on my leg that is growing out of a *hair follicle that is already taken*. Some might say that it was there first, but I refuse to believe such conjecture.

While painting my nails for the first time in ages this afternoon, I realised how helpful the act is for trichotillomania sufferers. Even if I was desperate to pick or pull at my skin, I wouldn't have been able to, unless I wanted to be covered in nail varnish. It's a shame that waiting for your nails to dry all day isn't a viable option. A bit of a pointless trich tip for you there.

I think I need to watch a few more of those ridiculous videos on YouTube where ingrown hairs are removed – some by doctors, some by complete imbeciles. I haven't decided whether those videos help me or make me more desperate to pick at my skin, to be honest. I'll let you know tomorrow.

Thursday 27th October 2016, 3.55pm

Last night I *did* end up watching a few of those ingrown hair videos on YouTube. No, they did not make me resort to hurting myself. I made it through the night completely unscathed, but I once more questioned the doctor's methods. With all their certificates and qualifications, they just didn't seem to attack the hairs or squeeze the spots right. I could have done it better – pass me a sterilised needle *stat*.

I seem to not be able to get enough of my breasts at the moment. This morning I flashed myself, *again*, and saw an ingrown hair. I was a little unprepared for the sight of it, as I thought they had all come out already. Like a true professional in my field, I have come to know the location of every single ingrown hair on my body intimately. I know how they'll grow and how they'll look when they come out. This one is new – or maybe due to the sheer volume of them now (*stop being dramatic Cara, there are about 15*) I simply forgot its existence. I keep looking at it and yes, I can confirm it's still there. I shall just have to stay strong and nurture it to grow like the others have. Leaving something to come out naturally is still completely *un*natural to me.

Like I've said before, I am writing this early because I'm seeing my friends later on. I'll be in too late tonight to report back. I am still adamant that I want to find a way of telling my friends that I suffer with trich, but I fear I'll chicken out at the last moment. I mean, I wouldn't ever bring it up as a surprise and say something like, 'Hey guys, how are you? I suffer with trichotillomania.' But if the right moment presents itself, I'll go for it. I'm hoping for an opening in which I'll mention it in a really casual way, then just pray that I don't see the look of horror on their faces. Wish me luck, dear Diary.

Help me?

Friday 28th October 2016, 6.43pm

I got in very late and was up early. As a result, I have spent today in some kind of walking coma, and I'm so tired I can barely move my fingers over the keyboard. So, how did I get on telling my friends that I suffer with trich?

Well, I completely forgot I even *had* the compulsion, let alone remembered the fact that I needed to try and get it into the conversation somehow. It didn't help that I was literally sitting next to my best friend's new boyfriend, who he was introducing to the group for the first time. He was fabulous, and I doubt I would have wanted to be remembered as the woman who said, 'Hey, it's great to meet you. I have trichotillomania.' I might have been able to fit in a quick confession right before dessert, but really, I had a great time. Trich was nowhere to be seen, which is as it should be.

In hindsight, I think a group meal in a busy restaurant in Covent Garden probably isn't the best place to spill my deepest, darkest secret to the world anyway.

Even though I was unsuccessful in my attempt to bring up the subject of trich, a lot of my friends mentioned how well I looked. It's something both my mum and I have noticed recently too. I'm not sure if it's in any way to do with trich, but my gut feeling is telling me it's because I'm starting to feel good in my skin. My scars are fading and the scabs are few, and it's like I'm a woman again. I haven't felt that way for a long time.

When I look in the mirror, there is a different expression on my face. God knows what the hell I'm talking about, but it's like there's a kind of inner peace seeping through. I think that kind of thing can show on the outside too, can't it?

I've just realised that it's Friday, and that means it's been three weeks since I started this journey. I know there have been incidents but instead of quitting, I've moved on from them. Pulling a handful of hairs out with my fingers and squeezing the odd spot is nothing in reality, but in the past, even those small actions would have caused all hell to break loose. I have learnt in these three weeks that guilt picking and pulling is by far much worse than a trich or derma slip-up could ever be. That feeling is never failure if you learn from it and move on straight away. I am going in a direction I'm proud of. I'm not perfect, but I am learning all the time and my skin is clearer than it's been for as long as I can remember.

I'm now falling asleep in front of my screen. Good night, dear Diary. I love you – and I think I love me too.

CHAPTER 7

THE TRAIN

Late 2011 and early 2012 was a particularly bad time for my trichotillomania and dermatillomania. It coincided with a very unhappy period of my life, both personally and professionally. All in all, I was a bit lost and didn't know which way to turn.

Around that time, I was living in Winchester with my mum. But my life – my friends and everything I knew – was in London. At first, I would travel in to see them as much as I could, but over the months, as my compulsions fed on my isolation, I saw my friends less and less. People asked to see me, but there were times when I'd made such a mess of my skin that the last thing I felt like doing was getting on the train to see anyone.

You could say that those wounds could've easily been covered. I could have hidden my scars behind a veil of make-up, and that way I'd have still been able to see my friends. But those marks were so much more than skin deep. They made me feel so low, as if I was trapped in a bottomless pit.

I felt like a failure; ugly, deformed, weak.

Being in this situation impacts how you interact with others. It makes you want to hide away and not see anyone until it all blows over.

I cannot tell you how many friends' birthdays, parties and social gatherings I have missed because of trich. It is exceptionally hard having a mental disorder which manifests itself physically. But even if it didn't, I would feel just as isolated. The mind is capable of making you believe anything.

I barely took that train to London by the end of my time in Winchester, and to this day it has changed the way I communicate with people. It has changed everything.

Saturday 29th October 2016, 4.04pm

Panic over; I located the black hair on my leg that I thought had fallen out – the one that is *growing out of a follicle that is already taken*. So, it is not only audacious, but also enjoys messing with my head. Where was it the day before yesterday when I searched high and low for it?! Black, bold hair on my leg, shame on you!

I noticed in the bath this morning that the scars on my stomach and breasts seemed a little redder than usual. I know, I know – I have no right to feel this way after the extraordinary amount of abuse my skin has suffered, trust me. But I couldn't help feeling a little bit sad seeing the scars so red and angry again. I know I don't deserve it, but please could they fade some more?

I'm still not feeling great today. It's like a lethargy has settled over my entire body and mind, and I am literally holding on for dear life until I can crash tonight in front of a Netflix marathon of *Stranger Things*. (*Even better*, I've developed a crush on the police chief, Hopper.) The show is so good and has held my interest so much that I haven't touched my skin once – I just want to touch the police chief.

I last used the tweezers on Sunday – so, nearly a week ago – and because I am failing royally at wearing my gloves (and can't seem to keep my hands off my face) I have felt more and more thick hairs growing back on my eyebrows and upper lip. I am less bothered by them now, though. I can feel them there and know that I'd rather like to get them out, but understand that I can't and it's cool. I don't think I would call it easy yet, but I'm getting there. Maybe it's because I know I can do it. I hasten to add that I'm still obsessed with touching my skin, and I think I can safely say that I am one of only a small handful of people in the world that has actually had a serious conversation with their own breasts.

This afternoon, as I was once more unable to control my temptation to look at them and touch them, I had a moment of realisation (again) about what I was doing. I actually said to my boobs, 'Now, Cara, remember what you have been doing. You've got to stop this. Come on now.' I still want to look at them, but I've kept them concealed from view within my top and bra ... for now. Oh dear.

I must dash as there is a pizza in the oven and I've got a date with Netflix and a rather attractive chief of police. *Fabulous*.

Sunday 30th October 2016, 6.00pm

I had a nightmare last night. I dreamt that I pulled out all of the thick hairs on my face that I have noticed growing for the last few days. It was unnerving because it felt so incredibly real – I could actually *feel* them being pulled out of my skin. I even experienced the relief and pure ecstasy of the act but, just like in real life, it was very quickly followed by a sinking disappointment. You can then imagine my joy when I realised it was just a nightmare and I hadn't broken my promise to myself.

But something unexpected happened. After realising it was just a dream, I had absolutely no desire to pull the hairs out for real. I still don't. Maybe it's because in my mind I've already got them. We'll see how long this lasts, as I obviously know the hairs are still there and this might only be a temporary respite, but I'll take that gladly.

It's hilarious how bad I've been with my gloves recently. Even as I'm typing this I'm not wearing them. They are actually next to me – so close, in fact, that they are tickling the side of my hand. I've moved them aside so it doesn't happen again. I feel that if I call it laziness I'm pushing it, even by my standards. It's more like there is a small part of me that still wants to touch my skin – but I don't care. Next week I have got to find a way to stop myself from doing it. Gloves or no gloves, the touching is what I've truly got to master if I stand a chance of being able to do this long term. So, here's my plan: find a way of killing the habit of touching my skin, but wear the gloves just in case so that I can't feel anything growing. So simple in theory, but the execution is tricky.

It's annoying because if I could actually stop touching my skin, I would be able to beat trich and derma once and for all. *Oh, why can't you stop touching yourself, Cara?!*

It's sad that I have been bloody lousy about wearing my gloves, because I know they help me so much. *It's not hard, Cara. Wear the gloves, don't touch your skin and you'll be okay.*

But I can't stop.

Why can't you stop?!

I think I will cease this inner monologue as I'm going around in circles. That's essentially been my life for so long: one big vicious circle.

Earlier, I looked at my stomach and saw that the scars had vanished. I know it's only temporary because I was cold and not doing anything, but it's nice to see something that has been such a rarity for so long: completely clear skin.

Dearest Diary, I truly think I am making progress.

Monday 31st October 2016, 5.22pm

Happy Halloween, dear Diary. So, you ask me: was it a day of trich or treat?

It was definitely a treat.

The only thing scary about the last 24 hours is seeing the amount of hair I now have on my body. And there are practically no scabs! I can't remember the last time that was the case, and I'm amazed by how far I've come. Ecstatic, even. My white cotton gloves have stayed on all day, so my unwitting costume this year is basically a mime artist.

I have always loved Halloween. I grew up trick-or-treating and have wonderful memories of dressing up and parties. But I have one not so good memory from Halloween a few years ago.

My legs were sore from picking them to bits, and so I hid them under thick, black patterned tights. I was at my friend's house and she decided to wear her legs bare, so she went into the bathroom to put fake tan on. I remember feeling a deep sadness that I would never be able to just decide, without thinking, to have bare legs. I have spent years hiding my legs, and any outfit that required a skirt or dress was meticulously decided upon well in advance. I know the exact denier of hosiery that covers scabs along with a good dab of concealer ...

I suppose I could have just taken off the tights and had a perfect costume already.

This year I have two tiny scabs on my legs that are about to fall off – and on their own too! I may have a handful of scars, but they won't keep me from my darling razor on the 24th November.

Last night passed by trich and derma free, but I did do a pretty big thing. I allowed Mum to tell my cousin that I have trichotillomania.

It was all casual, just a small sentence in a catch-up email that my mum sent to her. The exact words were:

"Cara is also in the process of getting over something she has had for over 16 years called trichotillomania and is happy with her progress."

See? Totally cool.

So, I have finally found a way of telling someone close to me about it. It feels good, I think – it's a little unsettling knowing my secret is slowly getting out there, but deep down I know it's the right thing to do. Ideally, I'd like to tell a few people who are close to me about it before I spill the beans and "come out" on my Instagram page. At present, I have 820 followers. I'm not going to lie, it scares me – so much so that my stomach just swooped. But like most things, I've just got to push through it.

It is my life and no one else's. This is part of me. It's definitely something I wish I didn't have, but hopefully soon it will just be a faded memory and not a monster on my shoulder, weighing me down.

Wednesday 2nd November 2016, 5.45pm

I have really found this week easier than I expected. Since Monday, it's been by far the best few days of this entire journey. I haven't been as good with the gloves today, but I haven't really touched my face so it hasn't mattered. I am sure it's just a good phase, but I don't think I've ever, in my 16-year trich career, been this blasé. My calmer periods in the past were never like this, and there were certainly no days on end when I didn't pull out hairs. This is new and I hope it sticks around.

In my quest to get this all out in the open, I was presented with an opportunity last night. I took it … kinda. A friend of mine asked how I was. I might not have mentioned trich by name, but I said I was "getting over something I've done for over 16 years and seem to be actually succeeding!" I even put that enthusiastic exclamation point in too.

Her response was lovely; she was excited for me. And in that moment, I felt excited too. There was an amalgamation of hope, forgotten possibilities, a life …

I think what I said was a fair summation of how I'm getting on. I know I could be better, but I could also be so much worse. On top of that, my attitude is changing. Tomorrow marks three weeks until my steamy razor date, and I'm already getting butterflies.

Thursday 3rd November 2016, 4.15pm

I have to say that I am absolutely fascinated with the complete 180 I have made. Also encouraging is the fact that the more I talk about trich in this diary, and the more I attempt to tell others about it, the less trich is this dirty thing and more just a part of who I am. Or *was* ... at least, I hope so anyway.

When I had been pulling hairs out from under my arms for maybe a year or so – I can't remember exactly when – I saw this woman on some reality TV show who pulled out her underarm hairs with a pair of tweezers *live on camera.* I think others saw her doing it and thought it was really weird, and they couldn't understand why she was doing it. Even when I saw this woman indulging in something I had been doing secretly for months on end, it made me feel a little queasy. It was shocking to see someone else doing this, after feeling like the only person in the world that did it. I had never seen anyone do anything close to it before. It was like looking in a mirror.

I know it's the most random memory, considering the magnitude of what my compulsion has become. But it always stayed with me, and maybe that's why I made that connection in my mind. Maybe that's why I've always thought of it as dirty. Who knows?

As per, after seeing her do that to herself, I made one of those empty vows, something along the lines of *thou shalt never pick or pull at thy skin again.* But of course, that night I was back in that bathroom pluck, pluck, plucking away like a guitarist playing a sad melody.

But it's not dirty any more, and there is no song.

Friday 4th November 2016, 5.00pm

I started watching the TV show *Homeland*, and it's fabulous. That is the only noteworthy thing to mention about last night.

Nothing whatsoever happened with my skin. I wore my gloves all night, but didn't need them because I mostly just sat there like a person who simply watches a TV show and doesn't have to think about their trichotillomania. It was refreshing not to even have the slightest urge to do anything. Like I've said before, I am sure this is just a good phase and I don't expect this level of blasé-ness to continue forever but I'll enjoy it while it lasts as it's all very new and exciting. I've never been this chilled out – especially as I know how many hairs are growing with wild abandon on my face right now.

This morning the only disaster that presented itself was when I got on the scales and realised I had gained weight, but my dismay came to an end when I got in the bath. As I had unintentionally left the light on, I looked at my skin – not for trich's sake, but for mine. I may have the odd scar dotted about, but that's it. I have almost clear skin. I can't tell you how crazy that is, because I know for a *fact* it's the best my skin has been in years. I think that moment when it dawned on me has got to be one of the loveliest, most peaceful experiences of my life. When I looked closer at the skin on my legs, I noticed a few ingrown hairs. But instead of even touching them, I accepted them for what they are. They are just hairs, and they aren't going to hurt me if they stay where they are.

It's funny, because my whole mental reasoning behind ever getting any ingrown hairs out was to make the skin nice and clear. When you go about removing an ingrown hair, you pretty much end up with the opposite effect, and it's almost always so much better to have just left it alone – and so I lay back in the bath and let the hot water glide over my body.

Today marks exactly four weeks since I started this journey, and I can't quite believe it. To an extent, pulling hair out and picking at my skin has always felt like it was out of my hands somewhat, like it was up to trich and derma as to how I'd get on. But I think I have finally realised that what I do to myself is totally up to me: *I'm* the one who decides what happens and *I'm* the one in control.

I am talking like this is something new and profound. In fact, it's only common sense. I knew it already, but I don't think I *believed* it until today.

As I pruned up in the bath, I felt so deliriously happy that nothing else mattered. All these self-imposed deadlines were bloody pointless. When I *finally* got out of the bath, I can't tell you how good I felt. Trich has had such a negative impact on how I have viewed myself and in the past, it has severely altered my perception of self.

Goodness, that bath was intense today.

I really can't believe how far I have come in only four short weeks. Screw the trich; I'm so happy. Back when I started all this, I didn't think I'd ever have such a fun, philosophical experience while submerged in bath water.

I have made a conscious decision not to write here over the weekend. Every single day since I started this journey I have written more than I ever anticipated I would, and at times it has taken over. But I know I need to cut off for a couple of days because I'm completely exhausted. I would like one weekend of nothingness. It's going to be strange not writing here for a few days, and I never thought in my life I would ever miss a Word document.

But I'll miss you, dear Diary.

CHAPTER 8

THE AUDITION

Once upon a time I wanted to be a performer. I got to the point where I was getting the odd job – I even had a (miniscule) following online, although really, I think it was over before it ever had the chance to begin. Those terrible years at secondary school made me believe I would never be good enough; as a result, I never pushed myself because I didn't think I could ever really make it.

Looking back, part of me wishes that I had fought past those feelings and really *gone* for it, but we'll never know what could have been. And now, to be honest, I'm glad. A career on stage and screen could have been wonderful and life-changing and given me an extraordinary life, but maybe it would have given me a whole new set of problems. Who knows?

During my time as a performer, I went to a fair few auditions. Once, I was invited to audition for a part, and the casting breakdown read: "Must wear a knee-length skirt in order to see your shape. No tights."

I panicked. Suddenly, the potential audition went from how to *get* the part to how to get *out* of it.

Illness has always been my go-to excuse. I mean, it's perfect: lie carefully, with the present situation in mind, and who'd ever question it? Who'd go to an audition with tonsillitis?! Unthinkable!

I was a genius when it came to tailoring my excuses to my needs. I'd had many years of training while suffering from trichotillomania and dermatillomania. And when I needed to appear in public, I had the ability of making even the deepest of gouges look like the most common of acne spots, with the right cosmetic tools.

There was nothing I couldn't spin to suit my situation – until an audition in which I was shortlisted for the role of the romantic lead in a music video. What they didn't mention at first was that I would be in the water and that my costume would show a lot of skin – my legs in particular.

I did an informal screen test and I remember the moment the "W" word was mentioned. There began a powerful constriction in my throat as I tried to exude confidence while feeling anything but. Suddenly, all I could think about was the infection I might get from putting my open wounds underwater – and they would certainly not want to cast someone whose skin was so badly damaged. This time I was trapped – I was already in the audition room. My mind went blank as I tried desperately to think of something to say. But I couldn't – I had no tailor-made excuses at the ready.

I cannot remember now how I got out of that particular pickle, but I needn't have worried as they ended up going in another direction, but that didn't bother me. What did bother me was the knowledge that I wasn't prepared and wouldn't have been able to do it, even if I wanted to. They could have got on their hands and knees and begged me, they could have doubled the money – and I wouldn't have budged. Money can't buy clear skin. Money can't buy freedom from your mind.

As much as I have wanted to be free of my compulsions, I've equally longed to be ready for anything – to be able to jump in the water at a moment's notice. I want to do anything I want to without being held back. And who knows? Maybe one day I'll be able to do exactly that.

Monday 7th November 2016, 5.23pm

It was a weekend of confessions. On Saturday morning, I was presented with an opportunity to tell my best friend about trich. And I took it.

I told him via text:

"There is something I haven't told you about me. Mum is the only one who knows. I have a condition called trichotillomania (I hasten to add, it doesn't affect the hair on my head) for over 16 years. I'm only mentioning it now because I think I'm getting to the point where I might actually be beating it."

His response was so lovely that I instantly knew I had done the right thing in telling him. Later in the day I wrote, as part of a post on my blog:

I've been working hard on myself and, also trying to deal with something once and for all, that I have lived with (secretly) for over 16 years. I do want to talk about it properly soon, but I don't think I'm ready to just yet. The only thing I will say about it is that, if I can get to a point where it doesn't control my life, I will truly feel free.

And I meant every word. I feel like with each confession I make, Trich loses a little more power. Soon it will be common knowledge, and Trich won't like that. It likes feeling special. It likes it when it is just me and it, locked in a bathroom with a pair of tweezers and a lot of shame.

Want to know if I actually did any damage this weekend, dear Diary? Nope. Did I touch my face at all and feel any stirrings of lust? Hell, yes! On Saturday there was a painful ingrown hair on the side of my face. I played with it a bit and tried to pick off the top layer of skin so that it would stop hurting. I haven't worked out if that is just one giant excuse or not. Well, whatever my reasoning behind it – whether it be honest or nay – the hair is still there. And, oh my goodness, is it thick! I think there might actually be *two* growing (*inhales sharply*), but I'm trying not to investigate too much as I don't think I can be trusted.

It's strange, but when I get to this state of hairiness I feel like I'm not clean. I know how bizarre that sounds but I'm wondering if that is another reason why I have trichotillomania in the first place.

On Sunday afternoon I wrote down my list of short-term goals. It's interesting – instead of wording them along the lines of "I will *never* pick again," like I have done in the past, I wrote instead:

"I want to get to the point where I am in total control of my trichotillomania and dermatillomania. I want clear skin and a regular beauty routine."

I think to write anything like "*never* pick again" is a recipe for total disaster. Sentencing someone with trich or derma to never pick again is never going to work. That pressure, that feeling of failure if you cave in and get just one hair, is impossibly hard. I have always ended up damaging myself more from the disappointment over my ridiculous, unobtainable goals than I would have if I had just been a bit more realistic about my expectations and understood what my compulsions are. I have come to understand more about them since I started this journey than I have in the previous 16 years.

That is not to say that I have a bloody clue what the hell is going on. It's more that I'm a little wiser than I was … I think.

Today marks exactly a month since I started this diary, and this afternoon there was the most perfect rainbow in the sky. Whenever I see a rainbow, even if it's in emoji form, I always feel a sense of overwhelming excitement, a warm hope. And so, to see one in real life – on a very important trich anniversary that I never thought I'd reach – is humbling. I feel more determined than ever to keep my date with a razor on the 24th of this month.

And so, dearest Diary, I'd better go now and put my gloves on before I touch my bloody face again. I love you.

Tuesday 8th November 2016, 3.34pm

Last night passed by in a lovely trich-free blur, courtesy of the last couple of episodes of *Poldark* season two (which once more reaffirmed the fact that I am definitely in love with Ross Poldark).

I know I have a hell of a lot of work to do before I can truly say that I am in control of my compulsion, especially now that I apparently have this ridiculous new obsession with certain ingrown hairs, but I am seeing so many positive changes every day. It's only a matter of time before ingrown hairs don't affect me any more.

'Mwahahah,' says Trich. 'That's what you think.'

Shut up.

I had a little bit of a blow this afternoon. Basically, someone mentioned on a YouTube video that you have trichotillomania for life and that there are only ever good or bad periods with it. When I first heard that I felt completely devastated and, for some reason, disappointed in myself. It was like being condemned to a life sentence.

I had a dramatic moment where I thought to myself, *what is the point of trying to stop when it's inevitable I'll just relapse again?* Luckily, that tidal wave of feelings was short-lived. And when I had taken some time to really think about it logically, I realised that what she said was probably right. But that doesn't mean I'm not going to try my best to get over it anyway.

I'm doing better than I ever thought I would, and so why shouldn't I hope for something more? It's my life, and no one gets to decide what I do.

While watching trich videos this afternoon, I came across another video that just required listening to river sounds for over an hour to overcome trichotillomania. Seriously, is this for real? Gee, thanks for that – we're all cured! Obviously, this person has never had it themselves. Or maybe they don't quite understand the compulsion enough to know that the sound of running water ain't going to do a thing – it'll do bugger all, to be exact.

In the spirit of desperation, especially after my obsession with a hair on my chin this morning, I thought I'd give it a go anyway. I listened to those river sounds for about two minutes before I was desperate for the bathroom ... I don't think it's for me.

After a pretty lengthy amount of time watching videos about trichotillomania today, I'm beginning to find it incredibly harrowing just to listen to people's personal experiences with it. It's odd, because at first I was totally okay with it. But now, when they describe some of the things they have done to their skin and hair, I find myself wincing. After a bad experience years ago when I had too much blood taken for some tests at the hospital, I now get an odd sensation in my feet if anything makes me slightly uncomfortable. One video I watched today actually made my feet hurt. Maybe it's because I know it could so easily be me. I think I might still force myself to watch them because when I do, I have zero desire to go anywhere near my own skin.

I know it's still very early in the day to do this, but I've decided to take the tape off the bottom of my trousers now, as my skin feels pretty irritated. I swear this isn't an elaborate excuse, and only time will tell if I use the time wisely.

Wednesday 9th November 2016, 2.26pm

So, the world woke up to the news that Donald Trump is the new President of the United States. I was surprised, to say the least, but even more shocking than that for me was the fact that I didn't end up doing any damage to my legs last night when the tape came off too early. All I did was watch some *Homeland* and an episode of *Father Ted* before bed. No trich in sight.

This morning when I was in the shower, I noticed that one of the scars on my tummy looked so angry (of course the light was off – I don't know what you're talking about ...). It's redder than I've ever seen it before, but I'll try not to think about the scar's existence too much, as it's like a reminder of how it all was before.

I keep telling myself how far I've come, but when my scars look like that, it's hard. It's still pretty red and – like my feelings for both presidential candidates – I'm confused.

I feel that the last issue with trich to tackle is the all-consuming desire to exterminate certain hairs and the inability to function until the hairs in question are out. Obviously, I have resisted the impulse for a while now, but in order to do this for a lifetime and not have to waste another second of my life thinking about it and fighting it, I've got to look even deeper within myself to get to the root (*inappropriate word use there, Cara*) cause of *why* I want to pull my hair out so much. Because I'm tired of it.

I've got 15 days until my date with a razor. I know that in that time I can really do extraordinary things. Well, perhaps "extraordinary" isn't the best word, seeing as I want to remain realistic with my expectations. But as the last 24 hours have proved in this world of ours, so much can happen in as little as a day.

Through my battle with topical steroid withdrawal and now this new, wonderful journey towards being trich free, I'm beginning to see this new person emerge. She's been hurt and broken, but she's still standing.

Thursday 10ᵗʰ November 2016, 4.37pm

I have not been wearing my gloves today, as I feel it's better that I just get used to the fact that I can't wear them in everyday life. I still need to find a way to master not touching my skin completely. I mean, the game is up: I know I'm turning into a gorilla and appear to be unwittingly growing a goatee now, on top of everything else I've got going on. I *know* there are hairs there and it's cool. I talk like I've been saintly with regard to wearing my gloves, but at this stage, not wearing them feels right. I'll continue to use them on the nights when my hands aren't busy typing on a laptop or something, though, because let's not push it now.

Tomorrow is a very big day for me: I am going to dry body brush everywhere. Did you hear that, dear Diary? *E-v-e-r-y-w-h-e-r-e* – and I can now, seeing as *there are no scabs left on my body!* This is a phenomenon, my Christmas miracle – something I thought for so long was an impossibility. I have been waiting for this moment for years. I am one step closer to having a beauty routine, and it's looking very likely at this point that I won't have to cancel my hot date with a razor.

Like with shaving, I've been scared to try dry body brushing or exfoliating for a long time, for fear I'd accidentally damage my skin and take off a scab too early. But now I haven't got any scabs to take off *because they're all gone!* They've fallen off on their own!

Tomorrow also marks exactly five weeks since I started this journey. Getting to this point has obviously changed me physically, but definitely not as much as it has changed me mentally. My self-love has had such a dramatic surge, especially in the last week. I barely recognise myself. I'm different, I see things differently and I am starting to realise that I deserve so much *more*. Faith – that flighty mistress that has been AWOL for such a long time – is slowly returning.

I really feel like I am changing, but the actual act of changing is so completely different to what I ever expected it to be. Now, I realise that change doesn't happen overnight. It is only when you have made the decision that you truly want to change that the journey of self-discovery begins. Change means that over time you evolve and grow. You still have to make mistakes and go off course, because that is the only way you learn. But you certainly don't just decide to change and suddenly become this perfect person. You have to map your course, and that takes time. I'm not there yet, but my path is slowly becoming clearer.

I feel like this experience has given me enough building blocks to grow a castle high into the sky. Every lesson I've learnt is a stepping stone that has saved me from drowning in the fear and thoughts of my past.

Sometimes, I wish I could start again, maybe as the 11-year-old Cara who was about to go to secondary school, full of wild, enthusiastic hope that this was something to be excited about.

I want to go back to a time before trich and derma, before secondary school, and lift that dull, heavy weight off my shoulders that I have been carrying for far too long.

The memories of that time will always be with me, but they don't have to define me like they have done for over 16 years. I've learnt I am stronger than I think, and that it's never too late to try. Taking time to achieve something truly great is the only way.

I've learnt not to listen to my demons or those who wish to hurt me, as I'm doing nothing wrong. I'm simply me, and dwelling on the past and fearing the passing of time gets you nowhere.

Believing in yourself gets you everywhere.

Friday 11th November 2016, 5.17pm

It's been a momentous, wonderful day today, because this morning I dry body brushed for the first time in my life. Oh my goodness, it was better than I ever imagined it would be. I felt like a woman dry body brushing her skin. I flicked that brush all over my body with such élan that I'm sure I took off at least eight layers of skin. Fabulous.

As I bent over to tackle my legs, I came face-to-face with my bikini line. At present, it is wilder than anything that's ever happened around that area. Hair on my bikini line, your days are numbered, my friend.

Really, it's not about the hairs that are there – they are what they are; a part of me – but I have craved the opportunity to have an actual beauty routine for years. I've wanted to remove body hair because I *want* to, and not because trich makes me do it.

I am still trying to wrap my head around the fact that I'm 100 per cent scab free – especially on my legs. All that remains in that area is a handful of scars, along with a few others that make a guest appearance if I stand for a really long time or get hot from the bath. But really, they aren't an issue and I'm probably the only one who can see them. Others probably wouldn't even notice them or care. I don't mean that in a bad way, but all of us are dealing with our own problems and people aren't going to care whether there is a random scar on someone's body.

Anyway, my legs are looking so clear these days that sometimes I have to do a double take before I remember they are my legs. It's a nice but very strange feeling after years spent intermittently hiding them from the world. *My* legs have been an up and down war zone since I started picking them in my teens and they have definitely been affected the worst by trich and derma.

I am still baffled how I have managed to avoid a single infection after all this time, but then again, I suppose with the sheer volume of antiseptic I have doused my skin in over the years, it's probably not *that* surprising after all.

Saturday 12ᵗʰ November 2016, 4.12pm

No trich, no problem.

Last night something unexpected happened. Pretty much straight after I finished my diary entry, one of my close friends sent me a message asking how I was. I took that to mean, "Tell me about your trichotillomania that I don't know you have yet."

I told her, writing a rather long and detailed message similar to the one I wrote to my best friend last week. Incredibly, she replied straight away and confessed that she has it too. She didn't know there was an actual name for it.

She even went into some detail about where she does it and why. What fascinated me was how casual her response was – as if it was just a part of her life; no big deal. There was no reluctance to tell me and no hesitation to confess, whereas I'd had to build up to actually writing the words "I have trichotillomania."

She just said it, and bloody owned it.

What made her response so much more surprising was the fact that I was so nervous to actually *read* it. Just like I was when I told my best friend, that fear of rejection reared its ugly head once more. I held off reading her message for as long as possible, until I couldn't bear it any longer and just had to see what she had said.

How amazing is that? With trich, I've always felt like I am the only person I know who suffers from it. But then again, if *I've* not let on that I have it, and I've done a pretty fine job of hiding it all these years, how do I know that other people around me don't suffer with it too?

Earlier this year, one of my friends briefly mentioned the word trichotillomania in conversation – I think she said something about having a slight impulse to pull out the hair on her head. It was all very flippant, and before I'd had time to process it, we'd moved on to another subject entirely. She actually used the "T" word, so maybe it's something a little less flippant than she's letting on. And just this week I remembered something else. I once had this friend who would always wear her hair in a side parting, because when she was younger she used to pull it out – only in a certain area – until it stopped growing back. It's odd, but I never once put two and two together and realised we shared this *huge* thing. I suppose trich is just this vast, changeable monster that can strike anyone at any time, and you are helpless to stop it.

Even though we are no longer friends, I wonder what would have happened if we had talked about our problems with trich together. I'm not saying it definitely would have helped, but it may have made me feel less alone and less inclined to keep it as some horrible secret. I might even have been able to nip it in the bud before it got out of hand.

Sunday 13th November 2016, 5.13pm

Last night I had a bit of a setback – well, that is what I thought it was initially. I had a spot on my leg that was very itchy. I'm not sure if it was a bite, but my mum had something very similar too. Not really thinking about it, I scratched it and accidentally caught the top of it with a sharp fingernail so it was sore and open. I tried not to freak out about it, but before bed I naturally started worrying that I'd have to reschedule my date with a razor. Even the thought of doing that after coming so far made me feel devastated. But as I lay in bed, I came to the shocking realisation that I was being absolutely ridiculous.

Trich: *You are a ridiculous human.*

No, I'm not.

Yes, you are.

I knew I just needed to calm down, and so I told myself all that mattered was that trich wasn't responsible. Besides, everyone in the world gets random scabs, and I should just be jubilant that this wasn't down to compulsion. It was only an innocent mistake. I looked at it this morning and realised that it's just a small, dark red dot that I'm hoping will be gone before my hot razor date in 11 days' time.

Unfortunately, it wasn't all rainbows and puppies after that – oh no. Over the day, I found I was feeling too happy, so I decided to panic about the spot again. This afternoon, I realised that this setback (yes, suddenly it became a setback again, and not a harmless mistake) had affected me more than I'd like to admit.

Mwahahaha.

Stop it – you don't own me.

As a result, I found myself touching my face a little bit too much. I feel like I'm slowly coming around, but I still need to understand fully that the spot is only a setback if I let it be one. For goodness' sake, it's not a setback. But when any damage has been inflicted, my mind has always dealt with it by tormenting me. *Well, you might as well create more problems now, darling, as you have ruined absolutely everything!*

Goodness, your mind hates you sometimes, doesn't it? I seem to be constantly working on overtime, thinking about approximately one million things I need to do and change in one go. But then, if I slip up or am unable to do it, I feel like a failure. I was barely in the bath for any length of time this morning before I had thought of four things I needed to write down. When the mental list reached eight separate things to remember, I had to get out so I didn't forget them.

I would love to be this free spirit who roams the land, unbound by anything. But I know I can't do that until I fight my worst enemy: me.

Something good to come out of this is that I haven't pulled or picked at my skin once since the beginning of spot-gate, so I know I must be getting there.

I went shopping yesterday and bought what every woman has at the top of their shopping list: a nose hair trimmer. I got it in the hope that I could use it to remove any random hairs on my body (not my nose), instead of pulling them out. I tried it this morning, but I seem to have exacerbated the issue further, and now the hairs all look thicker and more obvious. Fabulous.

Unfortunately, I think I've realised that I have got to pull them out, otherwise I'll be left with stubble, which looks great on a man's jawline. But it's not exactly what I want for my poor breasts, so now I need to find a way to ensure those hairs never become ingrown again.

Welcome to the mind of a twenty-something woman living life on the edge.

Tuesday 15th November 2016, 6.20pm

It was another blissful evening last night, involving a couple of episodes of *Homeland* season two and no trich. All I want in life now is to work at a company where I have a father figure like Saul. As of this moment, I feel totally fine again about the whole spot-on-leg-that-might-not-be-healed-before-my-hot-date-with-a-razor-on-the-24th-November issue. Whatever will be, will be (but it best be gone by the 24th – that's all I'm saying).

I now have three separate pieces of trich-related good news to share with you, dear Diary:

1. This morning I had to take a photo of my eyes for my Instagram account and I couldn't believe how fabulous my eyebrows were. They are thick, wild and untamed, just how I like my men. I was pretty happy with my eyebrows before I started this whole life-changing journey, but now I'm ecstatic. Next week, I'm going to be very cautious with what I take out, and that will probably mean I only get rid of a few hairs in between my eyebrows that serve absolutely no purpose to anyone. It's amazing what a difference good eyebrows make to your face. When I look back on photos of me as a teenager, and even some from my early twenties, it's like I have a different face.

2. Another piece of good news for a rainy Tuesday in November is that I have found an effective method to kill any compulsion I have *flat*. Now, every time I go to touch my skin, I ask myself, *is it actually worth it?* It makes me stop and think about what I am doing and what would happen if I pursued it any longer. This could obviously only be temporary, but for now I'll take it. And besides, everything we have is only temporary – high five to *that* philosophical sentence.

3. I am on a bit of a diet at the moment, and because of everything I have achieved on this journey with trich, I have decided that this time I intend to stick to my diet because I know I have the strength and willpower to do anything I set

my mind to. After lunch, I decided that I fancied some toast, which wasn't part of my original weight loss plan. But I was cool with it, as it's only toast. When I came to eat the toast, though, I realised I wasn't hungry in the slightest and I really didn't want it. But my head was shouting *eat the toast* because I'd already planned to have it.

It took a lot of deep thinking before I was able to tell myself, *you know what? I'm not going to have the toast, because I'm not hungry.* And so, I didn't have it.

I know it sounds like nothing, but to me it is *huge.* I have spent my life being controlled by all these ridiculous self-imposed rules. For example, if I pull out a hair, my mind says I must then go and damage my skin some more, because I have ruined everything. With food, I will eat a small chocolate bar and then panic that I have ruined my diet. As a result, I then eat everything.

If I just pull out the one hair and eat the single chocolate bar and then move on, there would be absolutely no guilt and no damage to my skin or body.

What I managed to do today was take back control from my destructive mind. It's dominated how I have gone about things for such a long time. It's a massive step forward. I still have a long way to go, but I'd call that a really satisfying personal victory.

Mwahahaha right back atcha, Trich.

Wednesday 16th November 2016, 4.04pm

Another night passed trich free and now I want Saul from *Homeland* to hug me.

Scab watch: *touch wood* it's looking likely that the scab on my right leg will heal in time for my date with a razor. The scab is hard and crusty, and I don't think it will take too long for it to drop off now.

Derma: *That's what YOU think, mwahahaha.*

SHUT UP!

I'm a little conflicted this week. I'm finding my head is filled with all these exciting things I want to achieve, but my execution is laboured and I'm feeling completely and utterly overwhelmed. Since starting this journey, I have done a lot of thinking about what I truly want to do with my life. In the past, as is my way, I've panicked and done a lot of things at once. As a result, I achieved absolutely nothing. Now, I'm going about things a little differently and taking time to dig deep and do some soul searching.

I think I have known for a while now that I primarily want to be a writer – I love it, and I do it more through need than anything else. I am also currently in the middle of a project that I'm completely passionate about, but there is also something else that has been building inside me for quite some time. It's a nameless, hazy image that is finally becoming clear to me. From all these experiences that have challenged and changed me completely, I want to create something that will help others, as I think doing nothing would be a waste. I have learnt more through these challenges I've been presented with than I ever thought was possible, and I want to build on that and continue to grow. I am still pretty clueless about how I'm meant to go about it, and if I told myself five years ago what I was thinking of doing, I would have laughed, reached for a pair of tweezers, and then cried.

It's crazy how different all our lives could be if we had simply taken another turn. I sometimes wonder what would have happened if I had never had trichotillomania or gone through topical steroid withdrawal, or the multitude of other tough episodes in my life. But then I realise, as I sit here typing this diary entry in a hot pink towelling dressing gown, that I'm glad I did, as I am the happiest I have ever been. If I had maybe taken a different path, right now I could be wildly successful, have a holiday home somewhere eternally sunny, and have a wonderful husband and three placid children, not to mention a dog we all adore ... but I could also be totally and utterly miserable. I now truly believe with all my heart that things happen for a reason.

Okay, I am going to take a deep breath and chill out after inflicting upon you that philosophical paragraph. I apologise profusely, dear Diary.

But I meant every single word.

Thursday 17th November 2016, 5.50pm

In exactly a week's time I'm going to feel the cool embrace of shaving foam on my skin, followed by the sharp kiss of the razor as it glides along my bare legs and underarms. It says a lot about my romantic history that I've never been so excited for a date in my life. I should maybe be more concerned that I'm even treating it as a date in the first place – but we are meant to be together! I have decided not to use the razor on my bikini line, as that is only courting disaster.

Scab watch: the scab on my right leg is continuing to heal nicely. I think through sheer force of will, I'll get that thing off before next Thursday.

This morning I noticed an innocent spot with a head on it near the top of my thigh ... but did I squeeze it? Hell, no! I told myself it wasn't worth it and just moved on – I didn't even have a moment of doubt. I think that over time, I am getting into a new habit with my skin, realising that touching it would be worse than leaving it alone.

You know what will be very nice from now on? To actually do stuff and just *live*. Trich and derma have definitely stopped me from doing so much in my life. For a woman in my twenties I have done comparatively little, a feeling that is only exacerbated by the fact that all I seem to read about is women my age leading *fabulous* lives and having all these *fabulous* experiences that they'll treasure forever, armed with *fabulous* stories that they will one day be able to tell their *fabulous* grandchildren. My twenties have been strange, to say the least. All this expectation pressures you to fit a certain mould that has been shaped over time. Sometimes, the rules of our generation are so rigid that you feel like a failure by default.

By now I feel like I should have bought my own seven-bedroomed house, had eight children and become a multi-millionaire ... and naturally have a dog as small as a petit pois.

I know I am definitely not blameless, though, and my mind has a *lot* to answer for. I have followed a mantra in so many areas of my life for so long that it feels like I've got to the point where I can only live or do something until, for example, I've lost five pounds or have clear skin. By following that pointless set of rules for years now, I have spent all that time waiting for a day that has never materialised.

So, I suppose you could say that I'd summarise most of my twenties in one word: waiting.

It's sad in a way to acknowledge that *that* is the word I would use ... but on the flipside, all that waiting has made me wiser. So, at 29, I can say without a doubt that through waiting I have experienced *more*. And my life is richer for it.

But I'd really like to be a multi-millionaire too.

Friday 18th November 2016, 1.02pm

Still trich free. Still loving Saul (and now Quinn) from *Homeland*.

Scab watch: After feeling cocky for the last few days that the scab would fall off in time for next Thursday. Now, I'm feeling *like it will be on my right leg forever.*

Today marks exactly six weeks since I started this journey. Those are 42 life-changing days I couldn't be more grateful for. As it's been a long week, I'm going to cut off early and curl up on the sofa with a romance novel, and I don't intend to move for the rest of the day, unless it's to watch *Homeland*, naturally. I still haven't hugged Saul.

Saturday 19th November 2016, 3.55pm

This week, as I am getting so close to the "finish line", I've been thinking a lot about why I haven't been able to do this before now and why I let it all go on for over 16 years. Surely, it would have been so easy to have stopped by now? All I needed to do was just take a breath, move my hands (and eyes) away from my skin and just say 'No!'

Then I remember that it's never that simple. I grew up with eczema, with the constant flippant remarks from others telling me not to scratch. Wow, did that annoy me. It's easier said than done when your body feels like it's covered in itching powder.

But then I suppose we're all guilty of it in one way or another. We see someone else's life and their problems seem so simple to rectify on the surface. But then why don't we implement changes for ourselves with our "trivial" problems?

It's never simple. It's anything but – and we can't possibly understand what is going on in another person's head and be able to judge what they can and can't do. In most cases, the mind is by far the biggest evil to defeat.

The condition I had for over two years – Red Skin Syndrome – was a little complicated. Most of the medical community – those you are meant to trust – treat it as something that doesn't exist. But when I searched on Google, desperate to work out what the hell was happening to me, I just knew with all my heart that this was what I had. At that moment, I made the huge decision that I was going to go down a certain path, go against the people I was meant to trust, and come off the medication that had caused the condition in the first place: topical steroids.

Living with that condition – especially through the times when my skin was truly horrendous – I was shrouded in doubt. Maybe all those doctors and medical professionals who were saying 'See? Red Skin Syndrome doesn't exist,' were right. Perhaps I just had eczema and the steroids weren't to blame. I had to constantly fight my own mind; it was telling me I was doing the wrong thing and that I'd never get better.

In the end I did, but the doubt was sometimes harder than t he sleepless nights of oozing and broken skin. It's odd, but when I look back on everything, I realise that I would never have been able to battle these other monsters, trich and derma, if I hadn't gone through all this trauma. I wouldn't have known exactly what I was capable of. I realised if I was able to grit my teeth, live through more than two years of doubt and come out victorious, I could do *anything*.

Right, I'm done for the weekend so no diary entry tomorrow. I need a day off from everything – even thinking – and it's amazing how revived I feel after taking just a little bit of time off today and yesterday ... along with the chocolate I had earlier. Fish and chips beckon. Fabulous!

Monday 21st November 2016, 2.31pm

I had a much-needed day off yesterday; all I did was sit on the sofa and read a romance novel with some mint chocolate. I wore my gloves because the thought of idle, bare hands for an entire day didn't seem like a good idea. I actually found it quite comforting having them on. I think I'll definitely continue to do that in the future, just in case. Now, my mind is focused on finding ways to keep this up long term. I'm hopeful I can do it as I've noticed, especially in the last week, that old habits are dying. I find myself in the bathroom naturally looking away from my skin, whereas in the past I would have had my eyes firmly planted on my bikini line or on my raised leg, ready for inspection. I don't touch my face much at all any more, but I can't lie and tell you that I'm not eager to get rid of the excess hair.

Scab watch: *It's* still hanging on for dear life.

I am finding with my dermatillomania generally that my desire for clear skin is by far outweighing my desire to pick; I leave spots alone now or squeeze them as little as possible before stopping.

I've been dry body brushing every few days and the difference in my skin in such a short space of time is quite astounding.

Things right now are so much better than I ever expected them to be. For so long I was scared of getting to this point, for fear that all I'd be left with is damaged skin. Why is fear so destructive? If you took it away, what would happen and how would you feel? What decisions would you make?

In a way, I was also scared that in eradicating trich and derma from my life, I'd be taking away my ultimate comfort blanket. It's all I have known for so long that the thought of not doing it leaves me feeling a little exposed. I'm absolutely terrified that there is nothing to break my fall. I fear, more than anything, that I have become one of those people that spends their life being philosophical every five minutes. For that I am truly sorry, dear Diary.

I've been working since six o'clock this morning, and I should really carry on for a little longer. But I've only got 135 pages of my romance novel left to read, and I must know if they get together or not!

I should probably say that I've already read the book. Three times.

Updated scab watch: About five minutes ago I looked at the offending thing on my leg – I *swear* I only touched it lightly – and ... *it fell off!* Underneath, the skin is slightly pink, but healed beautifully and I couldn't be happier! I can now get excited for Thursday in the knowledge that I am 100% *scab free!*

I am hairy and happy. What every woman should be before their hot date with a razor.

Tuesday 22nd November 2016, 6.56pm

It actually feels like Thursday will really happen and it's no longer just some painful fantasy. I have dreamt about this day for so long, but now that it's finally so close to being reality, I can't contain my excitement.

Now that I'm at this point in my journey, I realise how wrong I was about everything to do with my compulsions. A few years ago, I wrote a book called *Weighting to Live*, where I briefly highlighted the protagonist's battle with trichotillomania. As the book would definitely be categorised as women's fiction / chick lit, I changed the woman's battle with trich accordingly. When I wrote it, I think I genuinely believed that in real life there *would* be this lightbulb moment, and all of a sudden, I'd never want to pick or pull hairs out again.

Now I know it's a little more complicated than that. This isn't something you can just say goodbye to, no matter how desperate your desire to stop. I think, in a way, that I *did* have a kind of lightbulb moment on Friday 7th October, but the journey has definitely not been what I imagined it would be. That was when the hard work really began, and I have spent every day since fighting. Even though there have been times when I've given in – because I certainly haven't been perfect – I have slowly come to realise that the real victory against trichotillomania and dermatillomania is finding how to control it. I think I have.

I am going into Thursday with a new understanding about things. And so, I think, in that respect, I have won. The only thing I will have lost is you, dear Diary. Our time together is nearly over and you have become such a huge part of my life. I know I have to move on, but I'll never forget you and this life-changing time. Thank you, my friend.

Wednesday 23rd November 2016, 6.08pm

You know what? I have finally run out of words. I think it's because part of me has already moved on from it all. I spent last night and most of today in an excited haze. I kept thinking to myself, is *this really happening?* But now, it's finally dawned on me that this date with a razor is actually on.

It all feels wonderfully profound, but I must stop before I break into an inspirational song or something. I'll save any remaining thoughts I have left for tomorrow. I know I want to say goodbye to you properly, dear Diary, but now is not the time.

I would even like to say farewell to you, trich and derma. If it wasn't for the suffering you have inflicted on me over the years, I would never have learnt what I have about myself. It's all been worth it – the dark days, the fear, the pain. Thank you, thank you, thank you.

Thursday 24th November 2016, 5.11pm

I find that when you build up to a moment for long enough, more than likely it'll end up being totally different to what you imagined it would be – that's how it was for me today.

I will begin with what can only be described as the worst shave of my life. I was so out of practice that I missed whole areas and grazed myself in two places. But that's cool, because I totally have a beauty routine now!

The effect was still pretty awesome. I kept touching my legs and encouraging my long-suffering mother to do the same. Even my pyjama bottoms felt different post-shave. I'm used to the friction of a bit of hair, but today the material glided over my skin.

I didn't just shave my legs. I told all of my excess hairs on my body, 'It's not you, it's me,' and pulled them all out. I wanted to do it, but I can only describe the experience as utterly boring, underwhelming and painful. The removal of my moustache truly felt like torture. The eyebrow hair extraction (I didn't take many, preferring them a little more natural) felt like I was lashing myself with a miniature whip. And dear *God*, my breasts felt like they were being electrocuted.

Honestly, I did it all mechanically and looked forward to it all being over with. No longer shall I pull hairs out with relish. I think this has well and truly become a beauty routine rather than a compulsion. Fabulous.

I then proceeded to take photos of areas of my skin where trich had been my crutch. Looking at the pictures on my laptop was a little bizarre. Apart from the faint shadow of scars, I had totally clear skin. It's going to be an odd experience in the future, knowing I have nothing to hide and only a bunch of faded scars to keep me company. In the past, knowing that I was covering up this big secret was like a perpetual black cloud over me. That cloud has finally lifted, and I wouldn't be surprised if this whole experience turns me into a nudist.

In the afternoon, I "came out", as it were, and published a blog post. I also uploaded an Instagram photo where I said, in plain English, that I suffered from both trichotillomania and dermatillomania.

Just before posting the blog, I had a sinking feeling in the pit of my stomach when it hit me that this was the moment I was finally making it public. Yet that was nothing compared to what happened just before I hit "share" on the Instagram photo. At that point, my thoughts and feelings were bordering on unhinged. I was amazed by how much of a big deal it was for me personally. Coming clean is both nice and scary in equal measure. I feel completely naked, laid bare – just like a nudist.

The original Instagram photo and blog post are there for all to see. They'll never be removed. They are milestones which mark important moments in my life, and today is certainly that. It was only just before posting that I realised today is Thanksgiving in the USA, which seems apt. Here is what I wrote on Instagram, under a photo of my bare, shaved legs:

"There are moments in life that on the surface seem so small, but in reality are something wonderful. Today I had one of those moments: I shaved my legs with a razor for the first time in years and this is a photo I took straight afterwards. No filters or anything used. It is hard to put into words why something so trivial is a big deal for me. It is nothing to do with TSW [topical steroid withdrawal] and something only my mum had known about. For over 16 years

I've suffered from both Trichotillomania (a compulsion to pull out your hair) and Dermatillomania (a compulsion to pick at your skin). On Friday 7th October 2016 I decided I was going to stop, I was done. Since then the road has been far from smooth but after years spent making empty promises I knew this time, I wasn't going to give up. For years the two things I wanted more than anything was to stop using topical steroids and quit picking and pulling hairs out of my skin. I felt completely trapped by them but now I'm getting to the point where I can say that I truly feel free. I know I wouldn't have been able to get where I am today if it wasn't for going through TSW – it made me realise that if I can get through that, I can do absolutely anything. I know some of my friends / family who read this might be shocked but it's a condition you keep as close to your chest as possible – you feel ashamed of it, weak because to others all I'd need to do is just stop touching my skin, easy. Nope. Now it is no longer my deepest, darkest secret and instead, I hope it is a part of my past. I have written more about it on my blog today which you are welcome to read – link is in my bio. To my American friends, Happy Thanksgiving, I'm feeling pretty thankful myself..."

It's only been a few hours since posting, and already the kindness has been overwhelming. I've had comments and messages congratulating me, and even some private messages thanking me for my honesty and telling me that they have the same compulsions as I do. Part of one comment I received said "it always felt like I was the only one". That felt quite haunting to me. I think I have finally come to understand that none of us are ever the "only one", no matter how strange our "flaws" might appear to be.

So, now that I've gone and done this big thing, what happens next? Well, first I am debating about whether I should throw my electric shaver in the bin or not. For a start, it's really old and slightly broken now, but the main reason I want it gone is so that I have absolutely nothing to fall back on. It has always been my safety net, a way to get the semblance of a shave without disrupting the scabs I have created through my compulsions.

Apart from that, I will continue to dry body brush and shave until I find a routine that works for me – not because trich has told me to, but because I want to. What I *want* more than anything is to just *live* and stop feeling limited by what I think I can and can't do.

I want a life.

And so, dear Diary, it is time for us to part ways. I shall miss you immensely, and I will never be able to thank you enough for all you have done for me. You have come to know two people here: the girl who started this journey who was scared and unsure of herself, and the woman who is someone else entirely. She is still finding her way but starting to think a little differently.

I wasn't going to give you any more of my precious time, Trich and Derma, but I do want to say thank you for being a part of my life. Even though you have been responsible for me missing out on more opportunities than I care to think about, you have also brought me on this particular journey. Now, I am happier than I've ever been, and that makes me feel truly excited.

I have discovered a love of writing, which I might never have explored if my life had taken a different turn. And when I really think about it, if I had actually taken some of those opportunities you held me back from, I could be in a very different place right now.

I could be dead, who knows?

I hope you will indulge me in this last cheesy sentence as I can't help myself. Besides, I think it sums up exactly how I'm feeling right about now ...

Ding dong, the trich is dead.

CHAPTER 9

REFLECTION

I HAD A SECRET

The disorders that were once so shrouded in secrecy have been exposed and now lie open to the elements. From my diary you will already know that I told a family member first of my secret, followed by two close friends before a public Instagram and blog post on the subject. I shared a part of myself that had once been so close to my chest it nearly suffocated me. Now, I can finally breathe that my secret is out there. Six or seven years ago when my compulsions were at their height, I would never have *dreamt* that I'd be able to tell anyone, let alone write a *book* about it, available for anyone to read, and I cannot tell you how freeing it is to know that that part of me is no longer just mine. I mentioned in my tips that by simply admitting you have a problem dilutes its hold on you and now that my trichotillomania is out in the open, things with my compulsion have changed.

Now, I never bother mentioning dermatillomania as, for one thing, it's not really any part of my life and to be perfectly honest, even saying the word trichotillomania is enough to be going on with and is a conversation in itself – no one has time for that.

What I find interesting is that it is only in the time since signing with Trigger Publishing that I've openly discussed my compulsions. When I catch up with friends and tell them I have a book deal, they have naturally asked what the book is about and now, I just say it: 'I suffer from trichotillomania.' It is a part of me and nothing to be ashamed of. At first, I found myself hesitating before admitting it – skirting around the subject – but after a while, it was fine and it's incredible how many people I've talked to, some who I've known for many years, who have the same compulsion as me, no matter how big or small their problem with it is. This New Year's Eve, I even had a conversation with a friend about our mutual trichotillomania in which we exchanged very minor details on how and where we suffered from it. What's also fascinating is people's reactions to it. In your head, you imagine those you tell looking nothing short of revolted – maybe also making a dramatic statement along the lines of, 'What's wrong with you?!' – but the only physical reaction I've noticed has been a small shrug of acceptance, which makes you realise that it really doesn't matter.

Mentally, I feel pretty good about it being out there. Great, actually. I feel proud of myself and all I have been through. Even better is that it opens a dialogue for others to talk about their own problems, whatever they may be. We all live such singular lives, most choosing to suffer in silence as I did for so long, but by openly admitting you have a problem, it gives others the confidence to put their hand up and say, 'This is me, I suffer too.' We can all help each other by simply being honest. We can learn so much and as a result, grow. Bloom.

I did have a secret, but now I have freedom.

WHAT MY MUM "PICKED" UP ON

I have mentioned before that for a very long time the only person who knew even a fraction of what was going on was my mum, so I thought it would be interesting to hear, in her own words, how it has been for her – having to see someone she loves hurting themselves – because although we might be the ones that bear the physical scars, our actions without meaning to can impact the people closest to us. It is hard for me to read what she has said, but I think it is important to take responsibility and understand what I have done as I feel that is another step towards healing, both in body and mind.

"It feels strange to talk openly about this subject because for so many years it was a shared secret.

I had not come across the words trichotillomania or dermatillomania before, although I knew that trich related to hair and derma, the skin. I had heard of people pulling out the hair on their head and self-harming by cutting their skin, but didn't know about the compulsion to pick at the skin or pull out body hair, eyebrows, etc.

I think it started when Cara was about 12–13 years old. The first time I noticed it was when I walked into a room and saw Cara with her arm up, squeezing something in her armpit. I must have said something like, 'What are you doing?' She put her arm down quickly and I thought it was a one-off spot she was squeezing. I don't remember seeing her do it for a while but now and again noticed red marks if she lifted her arms up. I also started to notice her eyebrows getting thinner and red spots around them too. She was very defensive if I mentioned it, so I didn't say too much as she was having a tough time at secondary school, but I was very worried that her skin would be scarred or she would get a serious infection.

As time passed, things got worse at school for Cara and my mum was becoming unwell and she stayed with us a lot. Cara was very close to her and this added to the general uneasiness with everything. I came home from work one day and my mum said she had seen Cara picking under her arm. I hadn't said anything to my mum or anyone about what Cara was doing and I just thanked her for telling me. There were times when I felt desperate and wanted to tell my mum but didn't want to worry her. My mum had some tests and we were told she had lung cancer. She moved in with us, and I don't know the extent of the picking and pulling at that time because, looking back, it is just a haze but I remember smelling TCP every so often.

At some point, Cara started picking out the hairs on her legs. I remember one day I was working at home on the computer and Cara was sitting on the bed behind me. I turned suddenly to tell her something and saw both of her shins from knees to ankles were a mass of bloody wounds. I couldn't help but cry out and Cara was furious that I had seen them. I was so shocked by the extent of it that I was stunned. One of the hardest things is to watch someone you love hurt themselves and there is nothing you can do about it.

Cara had also been battling what she thought was eczema but on 6th June 2013 she found out about Red Skin Syndrome. She stopped using topical steroids from that day, and it took approximately 27 months for her to recover. It was so wonderful that she was finally free from a condition that she thought she would have for life. Cara had tried to stop picking over the years, but I think going through TSW has given her the strength to tackle other demons and on 7th October 2016, Cara told me that she was going to stop picking and pulling out her hairs. She said she was fed up with it and that it had become a habit rather than a compulsion. She kept a diary and by the third day, she was so happy because she told me that was the longest she had ever gone without pulling.

I can't believe two conditions that caused so much stress and worry over the years are no longer part of our lives."

MENTAL OR PHYSICAL?

What came first: the chicken or the egg? One of those questions designed to make us think for as long as there have been chickens or eggs.

Trichotillomania and dermatillomania might be classed as mental disorders yet manifest themselves not only mentally but physically. Although, for those who are predominantly habitual pickers and pullers, should they then be classed as physical disorders as some people are controlled by their inability to stop touching their skin?

When you are suffering from a mental disorder, all you want to do is hide away and shut out the world, not telling a soul that this part of you exists, but having something like trich or derma makes that impossible to do as it's branded onto your skin in the form of missing hair and wounds, unable to be covered. Having your dirty little secret out there for all to see, almost as if you have been turned inside out, makes you constantly feel as if you are under attack and vulnerable, with all eyes on you; searching for any weaknesses and reading your deepest, darkest fears and innermost thoughts.

You have a constant reminder of what you have done staring back at you, taunting you, and are unable to forget as the scars, wounds and bald patches won't let you.

Trichotillomania and dermatillomania are mental disorders but how could anyone know that when all others can see is hair loss and scabs? We are fighting not only our own minds but people's perceptions of our very misunderstood compulsions. You imagine those looking at us suffering and thinking, *just stop pulling out your hair / picking your skin if you don't want to do it, then.* Great, thanks for that.

With this book I hope I have been able to shed some light on two compulsions that are usually kept in the dark – as if I have lifted a rock, only for thousands of bugs to suddenly crawl out from beneath it – and show that they are not just skin deep.

SCARS

This section is in two parts which will detail both the physical scars I have, as well as the mental.

Physically, I would say I have been let off lightly; as I previously mentioned in my 16 month update, I have absolutely no scars on my legs, bar one which I have had for many years just above my right knee. My underarms are free from marks too, but I have noticed the skin is slightly stretched and prematurely wrinkled there, although that is a small price to pay for a situation I never thought I'd be lucky enough to find myself in. My face is free from scars too, and the only place I have any real damage is my breasts, along with a little mark on my stomach, but more on those areas later. I think what I feared more than the scars was damaged follicles from the near-constant abuse over so many years, but the only thing I've really noticed is that the hair under my arms is much darker and thicker now than it was before. I'll take that, gladly. Time may tell a different story but for now, this is more than I could ever have hoped for.

Now, on to my breasts and, to a lesser degree, my stomach. My body has not forgiven me for defacing those areas and although there are periods when the skin can be pretty clear, for the most part, it is not. That is mostly down to ingrown hairs reigniting old scars to come out and play. No matter how long I leave them be, I inevitably end up having to pick the hairs out in a desperate bid to try to stop the scars from being so red. Same with my stomach and there is an area, just below my belly button which every few weeks or so will come up angry and red until the trapped hair is released.

This is usually how I trigger my mental scars. Now, if I get any spot or blemish on my skin, it can send me into a panic and conversely, make me want to pick or pull more, seeing as I'm already "marked" – what's a few more spots to add to the mix? I'm aware it's a very strange mentality, and one I would really like not to have, as I do exactly the same thing with food: I'll eat a harmless piece of chocolate but suddenly, another perverse part of my brain says, *well, you might as well eat what you want now, seeing as you've ruined the whole day*. It's funny how a lot of us treat a new day as a fresh start when we could take the moment we are living in to begin. What is it about sleep that tricks us into believing the slate is wiped clean? The damage is still done from the day before, whether it is with wounds or food binges.

I find it very hard when those faded scars on my breasts and stomach come up as they take me back to a very bad place. With those scars I feel dirty, unattractive, and can see in my head all those lonely hours from my past spent in the bathroom picking and pulling at my skin. It can be all I think about, until the scars fade once more and I blissfully forget that I ever panicked in the first place … till they come up again.

Since my six-month update, three men have seen me *en déshabillé* and oddly enough, on the day I self-published this book in its original form back in June 2017, it was also the day man number one saw my breasts and bare skin for the first time – he was also the first human to do so in many, many years. I remember on the day a lot of the scars on my breasts were angry and I felt extremely self-conscious and panicky about them, but to put it delicately, he didn't care. There were moments with man number two when I had a few really nervous episodes with one particularly low point where I actually started Googling for heavy-duty body paint. Man number three wasn't around long enough for me to even have time to panic, but in our brief but enjoyable hours together, he certainly wasn't complaining. I think the worry of scars and marks that I have been obsessing over all these years has been a bit redundant. That is not an excuse to pick or pull, I'm simply saying that the areas we dissect and over-analyse in our head, which can be all-encompassing problems, are more than likely unseen by others. We imagine them to be so shocking, so terrible, that we almost see ourselves as swollen lobsters but they are just scars – we all have them, and you don't need to suffer from trich or derma to join that over-subscribed club.

Mentally, physically, we are all riddled with scars in one way or another and slowly, I am realising exactly that. Sometimes, you can say all this profound, enlightening stuff but not fully accept it yourself, even if you know it to be true, so I think it's going to take a few more years of self-discovery before I completely come around to the idea. But what I *do* know for sure is that even if I am not going forwards all the time, I am most certainly not going back.

REFLECTIONS

As a woman soon to celebrate turning 31, I have had a long time to form a pretty intense relationship with my mirror. Growing up, I never even thought about it, but when I went to secondary school, this piece of glass had a negative impact on my life. I spent hours in front of it every week, pulling at my eyebrows as a result of my trichotillomania, then my low self-esteem made me hate what I saw as a whole. And yet I would keep looking as if it was some kind of punishment. All the cruel things people said, I became in my reflection.

The mirror becomes redundant in the end, when you realise that no matter what it shows, your self-esteem would choose to see something else entirely, as if it was one of those distorted mirrors at a fun fair. Our minds are powerful enough to twist a reflection to suit what it wants us to see. Someone called me plain once, and when I looked in the mirror, it was as if all the details that made up my face were blurred until it met that description. You can step on the scales feeling slim, but if the number is higher than you anticipated, you can come off them feeling anything but slim. Then you look in the mirror and it's as if you're expanding in front of your very eyes. The mirror cracks in your mind.

Now, a little bug has come along and poisoned the minds of a whole generation, making us believe that the images we are bombarded with, day in day out, are real.

Social media. We look at people's perfect, unblemished forms, then look in the mirror and see the unfiltered, unedited version of ourselves and believe we are failing somehow. That we have done something wrong. We aren't good enough. We are different.

On the one hand, magazines will encourage you to celebrate and revel in your flaws, then on the other, they will offer you solutions on how to get rid of them. We are surrounded by contradictions. People who tell us to love ourselves and yet filter themselves to the point where they are no longer recognisable. Who are we meant to trust?

As a woman soon to celebrate turning 31, I have had a lot of time to reflect, and things that were blurred and hazy are finally coming into focus. Now, I look in the mirror and see me. I have scars, and cellulite and follicles because I am *meant* to have them. Now that the image is in focus, real, I choose to keep looking, because I've come to realise that there is nothing wrong with me for I *am* me.

Wouldn't it be lovely if we all looked in the mirror and simply saw ourselves?

I am not perfect or imperfect. I am me. I am not that girl on Instagram. I am me. I am not a walking filter and don't have cat ears and glasses that move when I blink. I am me.

I am not meant to be you. I am meant to be me.

You are meant to be you.

CHAPTER 10

THE LOOK

On a gorgeous, sunny day in July, I made my way to a date, feeling better than I'd done in a very long time. It was perfect. As I slowly walked up the street, with the sun shining down on me, I was at peace.

Until I got on the Tube.

That day I was wearing a beautiful navy knee-length dress. It was an off-the-shoulder floaty number which kept catching in the soft summer breeze. I could feel the delicious cool air against my bare legs. It was blissful, a feeling still so new and exciting after years spent hiding my skin behind maxi dresses and trousers.

When I took a seat on the train, I noticed a man staring at me. I ignored it at first, but after feeling his eyes on me, I turned towards him. I realised he was looking at my legs.

Suddenly, that dress became nothing but air. I felt naked, stripped bare. In that moment, I had forgotten everything I had been through and overcome. I was back in that locked bathroom, picking at my legs until they bled. My wounds were back and I had just imagined it all. Now, I was caught on a stifling Tube carriage, too scared to look down.

Finally, the man got off. Only then could I bring myself to look down and check my legs. I had to really stare for a few moments before I truly realised that the ghosts had gone. My legs were unmarked. I was free.

I went on that date in the knowledge that I had clear skin after too many summers of suffering in silence.

The weather was beautiful. My legs were bare. And I was no longer hiding.

CHAPTER 11

TIPS AND ADVICE

Since admitting online that I suffer from both trichotillomania and dermatillomania, I have received a lot of comments and messages from others asking me for tips that might help them too.

I have thought a lot about this, and I realise there isn't one clear-cut answer – more a collection of things I applied to my life that together have really helped me. In the past, I'd seen people dishing out advice to use toys and such to play with so you keep your hands busy but tips like that always felt like a disaster waiting to happen – I mean, there were times when I used to fantasise about being put in a straightjacket to physically restrain myself from getting at my skin, so when you throw in the suggestion of a damn toy, it ain't going to cut it. Let's be real, though – if I had been given the wonderful opportunity of wearing a straightjacket for a period of time, but also knew there was a hair that I needed to get out, somehow I would have acquired superhuman strength and ripped the straightjacket off to pull the offending hair out. This is to say, really, that it takes a lot to deter someone from picking or pulling when they are in the zone – and if you suffer from trich and / or derma, you'll know *exactly* what I'm talking about.

I think before I continue, I feel I need you to understand that these tips aren't a miraculous cure, and your days of trichotillomania and dermatillomania are not necessarily numbered. These are just some suggestions that have helped me reach this point. I have been pretty much scab free for a number of months now and have *an actual beauty routine* where I can freely shave my legs. Trust me, even saying something like that still feels pretty surreal. I've wanted this badly for years.

I shall continue to apply the following tips to my life, so that I can hopefully continue to stand victorious over trich and derma. Yes, this is something I'll have to work at for a long time but think of it like a diet: you do all these things to lose weight but that doesn't mean at the end of it you can go back to eating all the junk food. You need to find some kind of balance that you can maintain and live with for the rest of your life.

These tips come from my own journey and trich / derma problem areas in mind – which is pretty much anywhere but the hair on my head – and I have split the tips into two categories: physical and mental. There are fewer physical tips than mental, because I truly believe that the real work, like most things, is done in your mind – especially if you want a chance of succeeding. At the end I have also included a list of things that on the surface might appear to be obvious, but to anyone dealing with either trichotillomania or dermatillomania (or both, like me), they are philosophies that must truly be learnt from scratch. They might save you time.

To anyone reading this, I really hope these tips help. But trust me, I understand how hard it can be to stop. Having trich and / or derma is not a trivial thing – it can be this all-consuming monster that feels like it is drowning you.

PHYSICAL

Wear cotton gloves

Normally, my trichotillomania and dermatillomania starts more out of habit than anything else. I'd mostly do it without thinking, and by the time I'd realise what I was doing, it'd normally be too late. Inevitably, I'd have found something that I wanted to get out or investigate. With that being said, the first port of call for me was to keep my hands covered up as much as possible, because my weakness is the feeling of something jarring under my fingertips. I found cotton gloves immensely beneficial, as it meant I could touch my skin but I wouldn't be able to feel anything, as I had this barrier of thick material covering my trich / derma-hungry fingers. They are hard to keep on all the time if you are using a computer, though, as they tend to get in the way. But I find them to be immensely helpful when I am watching something and my hands aren't busy.

Wear clothes that make it impossible to get to your skin, or wear something on your head that makes it hard to get to your scalp

One of the places I have attacked the most is my legs. They have taken such a bashing and I am amazed that I only have a handful of faded scars left. When I was serious about stopping, I knew that I needed to find a way of making it impossible for me to get to my legs. In the past, I'd tended to pull up the leg of my pyjamas / trousers easily – again, without thinking – and my eyes and fingers would get to work. As I primarily worked from home back then, I spent a lot of time wearing pyjamas (yes, I am one of those people) but as they all had loose bottoms (pardon me), I would take some Sellotape and wrap it around the bottom of each leg. That way, I wouldn't be able to roll the material up easily and my laziness would override the impulse. Tights are also the world's biggest faff and work just as well, making it harder for you to get to your skin. Over time, some people will find that they won't bother trying in the first place. Polo necks are great too if you have an issue with your breasts – basically, try wearing clothes that are a lot of bother to take off.

Some people who suffer with scalp pulling often try things like wearing hats or bandanas during the day, in order to restrict access to their head. None of these things are fool-proof, but they can help combat the urge.

Watch videos of others going through trich

I may not have joined any forums or online trich / derma communities (which I know are very helpful for some sufferers; for example, there are many Facebook groups in which people share tips and tricks to deal with trichotillomania), but I did watch a fair few videos of others who had trichotillomania. I found them immensely helpful, especially the YouTube channel *TrichJournal*. Run by a woman called Beckie, she talks as if she is looking into my mind and verbalising my thought process before, during and after pulling / picking. Her videos are raw and thought-provoking, and everything I needed to hear. When I watched them, my desire to pick or pull decreased *significantly*.

Make a photo collage of people with clear skin and / or thick hair as a sort of goal

Regardless of whether it was a film, magazine or TV show, I'd always feel such a concentrated sense of sadness and regret if I saw another woman with lovely skin. But sometimes it would also temporarily stop me from doing any damage to myself. Back in October, when I decided I was serious about stopping, I created a little album on my laptop filled with photos of women who I thought had fabulous skin. When I really struggled and just wanted to pick or pull something, I'd look at this folder and it would sometimes control my urge to do it.

Take a deep breath and put your hands in a Chandler Bing Pac-Man claw

I know this sounds very odd, but if you aren't sure what I'm talking about, Google "Chandler Bing Pac-Man" and you will understand what I mean. Alternatively, think of it as if you are holding your fingers as though you are Catwoman. I don't know when I started doing this exactly, but I found that when I put my hands in a claw-like shape and took a deep breath, sometimes the urge to pick or pull would completely die. Putting my hands in this shape sends the oddest sensation up my fingers and arms. It's very strange indeed, but give it a go to see if it helps you.

Turn off the light in the bathroom

I hasten to say, do not put yourself in any danger. Standing in a dark, slippery bathtub or shower cubicle is only courting disaster. But every time I remembered to turn the light off, I would leave the door to the bathroom ajar just so that there was enough light to see what I was doing and not run the risk of slipping to my death, but it was also dark enough for me to not be able to see anything on my skin. In the past, the bathroom was a literal trich / derma playground for me – a place I could lock myself away under a bright light and just go to town.

Have a healthy diet

This is more a tip to help your scars fade and keep your hair thick and strong. It might be more down to genetics, but I have always had fast-healing skin, and I am amazed by how few scars I have for the amount of damage I have done. I truly believe it is down to food. Even though my love for pizza and chocolate knows no bounds, I have always had a pretty healthy diet that is high in oily fish, avocados, blueberries and broccoli – skin food. In the last year especially, because of going through TSW, I have made my diet better still, and now my scars and scabs heal even faster.

Keep your hands busy with other objects

Even though I don't think it is the right treatment for me, there are a lot of innovative gadgets out there, especially for people with trich. But one thing that many trich and derma sufferers find useful is having an object with which to self-regulate. Examples include fidget toys (including cubes and spinners) and stress balls. Keeping your hands busy with sensory objects can often mean you're too occupied with something else to pull.

MENTAL

You have to really want it

This sounds like a bit of a no-brainer, but I think sometimes there is an odd sort of comfort and familiarity where trich and derma are concerned. Sometimes, there is almost a reluctance to stop because of the memories of those blissful moments leading up to picking and pulling. They give you purpose, a feeling of being totally in control and so very secure. You then bask in the warm, contented glow of getting something out of your skin. You feel complete ... for a moment, at least, before you realise what you have done to your skin. At times, the wounds you have inflicted upon yourself can feel like they have come out of nowhere; you think to yourself, *how did that happen?!* It's like a drug: you want that satisfaction, the buzz, and you don't want to come down and have to see the reality of it. There are times when I have spent hours picking and pulling and been left with this absolute emptiness after I have done it.

On 7th October 2016, something changed, and I finally really wanted it. I had been building up to it for a long time. I just felt totally and utterly fed up, bored, frustrated – all of it. And I knew that this time I *had* to do it. I didn't want to have to spend my life hiding my skin, letting it rule what I could and couldn't do. I wanted a free life, and I was ready to do anything to stop.

Even now, there are moments when I still want to take the easy option and pick or pull something for the sake of it. I want to return to the warmth, comfort and familiarity. But you have just got to push past those feelings and remember *why* you are doing this. If I wasn't totally committed to stopping this time, I could have been wearing the thickest cotton gloves known to man and yet, still nothing would have kept me away from my skin. I really wanted this. And not only that, I wanted it entirely for myself.

Understand that trich and derma are not your friends

Continuing on from my last point, trich and derma were these omnipotent forces that I turned to through the good, the bad and even the times in between when nothing was happening. They were my security blanket. They feel like they are your friends, but on the contrary, trich and derma couldn't care less about your feelings. They don't want to help you; all they want to do is hurt you and make you feel bad about yourself.

Pause

Before you pull a hair out or pick a spot, ask yourself why you are doing it. Think about how you will feel afterwards and what will happen to your skin or hair when you have taken that irrevocable step forwards. Visualise the wounds you will create; the red craters on your skin, the bald patches, the total numbness you'll feel. It's never worth it.

Don't suffer in silence

Trichotillomania and dermatillomania are not things to be ashamed of. They are not there to make you feel dirty – they are simply mental compulsions you suffer with. I believe that trich and derma thrive on the secrecy we tend to keep them wrapped in. We are ashamed that we can't control ourselves, so we keep it as close to our chests as possible. But by getting them out in the open, they no longer fester. They are no longer allowed to grow into something bigger or harder to manage. Trich and derma are needy – they want you all to themselves. And so, by admitting that you have either or both compulsions, you are weakening their hold over you. You are also opening yourself up to further support and tips and advice if needed.

Neither trich nor derma like exposure much; instead, they want to feast on the darkness. For years, my mum was the only person that really knew I had the compulsions, but when I decided to really try to stop, I slowly told more and more people until it was completely out in the open. It was empowering. I felt strong and in control. And now, to make sure that no one ever doubts that I have it, I have a whole section on my blog dedicated to the subject. It's almost as if I'm saying, 'Yes, I do have it … and?'

Take control of your skin and hair

Always be aware that it is *you* who is the one in control of your skin and what happens to it – not trich or derma. It's *you*!

Make yourself aware of it every single moment of the day

I tried to be conscious of my compulsions as much as possible in a bid to stop myself from slipping into old habits. Previously, if I had started touching my skin, it'd normally be too late. I'd already found something I needed to terminate a.s.a.p., and nothing in the world would have stopped me. I think that was the worst part for me: the habit was so ingrained that I did it without thinking and inadvertently sabotaged my own progress.

If you feel you need to, seek the help of a counsellor, therapist or doctor

Treatment at the hands of medical professionals cannot guarantee that you will stop, and there are no current medications designed specifically to combat it. However, CBT or other forms of therapy might help you identify the triggers for your trich, learn how to keep track of your habits, and attempt to replace them with more positive ones.

We are all human

Finally, I think the most important thing to understand is that everyone has their own personal demons, so *never* feel like the odd one out. If you were to take just one thing from this list of tips, it would be to remember that everyone is fighting – some of us just know how to hide it a little better. We live in an age of social media and Photoshop, where everyone looks perfect and appears to have perfect lives. They are not real, and behind those images lie something very different indeed.

THINGS I SHOULD HAVE KNOWN, BUT DIDN'T

- Keeping your compulsion(s) a secret is never a good idea. Like I said earlier, these kinds of things feed on isolation.

- Everyone has little quirks. There is nothing to be ashamed of.

- There is no magical cure for trichotillomania and dermatillomania. They are compulsions which are very hard to get rid of. You just have to find a way to live with them and not let them impact your life.

- Getting out just one hair is a bloody myth.

- Hairs are not the enemy. They are a part of you, and they are there essentially to protect you.

- It's okay to leave a hair alone – it doesn't bite you if it stays where it is for too long. Nothing will happen; it will just continue to grow.

- Picking or pulling something out is only a setback if you let it become one. That isolated slip-up is nothing compared with the damage you do through guilt when you think you have blown it. Setbacks aren't setbacks if you learn from them and don't tell yourself you've failed.

SOME TIPS AND ADVICE FOR FRIENDS AND FAMILY OF TRICH SUFFERERS

- Be kind. Always.

- Never assume that getting better is as simple as taking your hands away from your skin. It is about as simple as a Rubik's cube.

- Whatever you do, do *not* tell someone not to pick or pull, unless they specifically ask you to. Often, tough love is pretty much the worst thing you can do to help those suffering with trich and / or derma. I can imagine it must be very hard seeing someone you love damaging themselves, but it will only make them feel worse if you try to be strict – a sufferer will panic and, in some cases, it will make them want to pick or pull more. You can kindly remind someone of what they are doing as there are some, like myself, who have compulsions that are predominantly habitual, and they might not even realise they are touching their skin in the first place. Some people will be grateful you told them, but you must have a conversation about this arrangement first. We're fragile, so please handle us with care and realise that the only person who can truly make us stop is ourselves.

- Even if you don't understand the compulsion(s) yourself, don't act as if they are something odd or weird. We already feel isolated, so don't make us feel like we're even further outside of reality. Do not judge something you don't understand yourself.

- Educate yourself. There is now so much information on both trichotillomania and dermatillomania out there – forums, websites, Facebook groups ... the list is endless.

- Be there. We are complicated and scared, and a hug can go a long way.

I want to finish this chapter by giving some advice to anyone who thinks they might have either disorder, or the beginnings of one:

No matter how big or small your compulsion(s) may be at this stage, do *not* – and I repeat, do not – do what I did and keep it to yourself. Run, run, run as fast as your feet can take you to the doctor – or better yet, get some counselling. Or both. I do not claim to be an expert on trichotillomania or dermatillomania, but what I *do* know is that keeping everything bottled up is a mistake. These compulsions can take over your life if you let them – they can even end your life if they cause you enough distress. Your mental health is just as important as your physical health, and we have both the mental and physical scars to prove it. These compulsions can be serious, and we need to treat them as we would any other illness. Do not leave them to fester, as they will only get worse. But always remember there is hope.

Like I said before, we live in an age where all the information you seek is at your fingertips. There are websites, forums to join and people you can meet who will understand you better than you understand yourself. You are never alone, and there is help out there if you truly want to find it.

CHAPTER 12

SIX MONTHS LATER

If I were to sum up the last six months, I would say I have been good. But that doesn't mean I've been perfect and there have definitely been some slip-ups along the way. For the first three months, I was fantastic – my skin remained clear and I had absolutely no desire to pick or pull whatsoever. But as time passed, I found myself slipping into old habits, and instead of acting on obvious warning signs and nipping them in the bud, I very nearly let things get out of hand – especially on my face, chest and torso. I don't think it was even down to stress; it was more that I was so used to touching my skin that I did it without thinking.

And before I knew it, I was back on that hamster wheel and couldn't get off.

I then started panicking that I couldn't stop, making everything 10 times worse and perpetuating the cycle. What's interesting, though, is that in the moments where I have struggled, I've actually found myself using my own trich tips (that I have included for you in this book), which have so far never failed to help me rein in any urges and get me back on track. I can live with that because there has been minimal damage, and I do believe that these last six months of fine tuning what works for me have been just as important as the time I wrote my diary late last year. I have learnt more about the warning signs to look out for, so I am able to deal with any issues before they are allowed to develop into anything serious.

Something I have found a little hard to deal with is the reappearance of certain scars that I thought had gone for good, especially those on my breasts and torso. But regardless, I'll gladly take those scars over any of the wounds from my past. Sometimes, the scars bring back certain memories that can be incredibly tough to have to revisit. In a split second, I can feel as if I am back in that locked bathroom, spending hours in isolation. But I refuse to let these memories affect my life, and they should only really remind me of just how far I have come.

What's ridiculous now is that I get really upset by any blemishes or scabs that have absolutely nothing to do with my compulsions. I feel like I've earned this clear skin. *Please don't give me something that I have to wait for to heal.* I'm trying to accept that there will be wounds and spots and scratches that are out of my control along the way and it's just a normal part of life.

One area that has really amazed me is my legs, which have gone from strength to strength. Not only have I kept up my shaving routine, but the skin is so beautiful. I have nothing to hide any more, and now they are just a pair of unmarked legs. Any remaining scars appear to be fading more and more over time. I can't wait to be able to finally show them off this summer – no more nude fishnet tights and maxi dresses out of necessity!

My legs, eyebrows, underarms and bikini line have remained untouched for the last six months, and my desire to pick or pull anything in those areas is pretty much non-existent. My dermatillomania has not resurfaced at all, and if I see a spot or any irregular lump, the desire for clear skin always outweighs my desire to pick. That is incredible.

In the last couple of months, I have also been making more of a conscious effort to date. If I'm perfectly honest, I am quite happy on my own. *You burn that bra, Cara.* But I do believe it's important to at least be open to the idea of dating and meeting new people. Even though I haven't yet met anyone with who I want to take things further, what's thrilling to me is that I'm not bothered if anyone does see my skin as I'm not waiting for anything to hurry up and heal. Even though I do have scars, I am comfortable enough in my own skin to not let it affect me.

If anyone reading this is finding it hard to see past their own scars, always remember that everyone has them. Whether you have trichotillomania or not, we all have a past – but our future is still up for grabs. I have found that the most attractive people in life are those who have respect for themselves and don't care what anyone thinks of them, and it doesn't matter what the hell they look like. I am still trying to love myself, and that is definitely a work in progress. But I'm getting there, bit by bit, scar by scar.

All in all, my future with trich looks extremely bright. I am now fully aware of the warning signs I need to act upon before they are allowed to turn into anything bigger, and I am taking precautions where possible, like wearing cotton gloves when my hands aren't busy. I am doing the best I can and I am hoping, over time, that any remaining urges will fade until they are nothing but a part of my very colourful past. I am not saying that there will ever come a time when I *don't* have trichotillomania, when it is just a compulsion I *had* rather than have. I am sure I will always have some kind of desire to pull at my hair, no matter how big or small, for the rest of my life. But that's okay; I have come to accept and understand myself a little better.

Understanding is key, in order to deal with so many of life's problems. As part of my diary on the 8th November, I talked about my fear of relapsing in the future. Well, here I am in the future, and I have no fear. I feel calm. I am not perfect, and I don't aspire to be.

There is light at the end of the tunnel. The wattage is a little duller at times, but have the faith that you can do anything and you will. I promise.

CHAPTER 13

SIXTEEN MONTHS LATER

I am writing this on the evening of Tuesday 13th March 2018, wearing M&S pyjamas, reflecting on just how much has changed in the last 10 months. To be honest, I don't know exactly where to start as so much has happened, it's quite overwhelming. I suppose I should "pick up" where I left off.

I think it's safe to say that dermatillomania is no longer part of my life. Now, I'm not really fussed about any spots or irregular lumps or bumps on my skin, because I can see them for what they are, knowing that on the whole they just aren't worth it.

However, I feel like my trichotillomania is a different story. Now, it's as if Trich is lying dormant, waiting like molten lava deep down inside, but solidified on the surface by my cool resolve. Although I know it is always there, I also know it's very different to the Trich of two years ago. I think I will start with the not-so-good news and finish with the wonderful.

The not-so-good is that I still have moments of weakness. If I was a guy, I'd definitely be a breast man, as it is that part of my anatomy that still gives me problems. The hair there is not like normal hair, which I believe is a result of using topical steroids for so long, and I have a lot of ingrown hairs in this area. Even though I do my best to leave them alone, the skin gets redder, more irritated and raised, and I find myself caving in and picking slightly to get them out. It's my *Sophie's Choice.*

That being said, this habit is not even a fraction as bad as what it was before. Unfortunately, this part is out of my control when the scars and memories of my past rear their ugly head. I find that that's when I am most vulnerable to having some kind of setback.

If this didn't happen, though, I do feel that I wouldn't have a problem at all. So, I suppose you could say that's still pretty good going.

It's weird; I was going to talk about other areas of my body where trich is still prevalent, but there aren't any. If I inadvertently feel a hair on my face, for example, but it doesn't come out easily, I simply won't do it and will instead wait for it to grow a little longer. You could ask me why I don't just leave the hair alone, but the desire to get rid of these hairs is now borne of vanity (or, to put a more positive spin on it, out of a desire to look good) and nothing to do with compulsions. I am simply pulling out hairs I don't want in order to look a certain way.

I don't tend to bother touching the other hair on my body at all now. Wow, I really have changed, haven't I?

Honestly, I think that at this point, if I let Trich back in, it's simply because of muscle memory as my body is so used to the habitual desire to touch, to feel, to pull. I have definitely also noticed that if I get upset or stressed, my desire to pull is stronger. Trying to undo more than 16 years of doing something every day, multiple times a day, is the real challenge.

Now, moving on to the wonderful.

Remember how I mentioned in my last update that I couldn't wait for summer to show off my legs? Well, I did just that, which felt strange and all kinds of wonderful. But there was still a part of me self-conscious about it. At times, it almost felt as if I'd left the house with no clothes on. Exposing my legs without fear was nothing short of liberating, but I would sometimes have to check they were indeed okay and that there were no marks. Now, my legs are my pride and joy, and by far, the biggest success of this whole journey. Never in my wildest dreams did I ever think that one day I would actually have them bare or even be able to shave them regularly. I treasure them now, and know with all my heart that I will never touch my legs again. I know that's a pretty strong statement to make, but it's true. And I believe it's down to the practices I put in place during the time I wrote my diary. I look at my legs simply as legs, and can't even remember how it felt to want to pick or pull there. It's fascinating how fickle the mind is and how it can adapt to any situation. Even better, some kind and wise skin god has decided to not give me any scars on my legs. How and why this has happened is baffling, but I'm certainly not complaining.

I think it's safe to say that I dated my way through last summer. At one time, I had a date with someone new every day of the working week. Dating has not been without its hurdles, though. Around this time, I also moved back to London to live with my best friend, and so far it is exceeding all expectations. I got a fabulous new job too. All in all, I have really been making up for lost time. My twenties were a strange decade where nothing really happened, and I'd like my thirties to be anything but that.

Even though I have made no secret of the fact that I want to write for a living one day, never in my wildest dreams did I actually think that a wonderful new publisher who specialises in mental health would want to publish my little diary. It goes to show that every cloud really does have a silver lining.

INFORMATION ON TRICHOTILLOMANIA (HAIR PULLING) AND DERMATILLOMANIA (SKIN PICKING)

What is trichotillomania?

Trichotillomania (TTM) is an under-researched and, in many areas, poorly understood mental health condition that revolves around hair pulling. While TTM has often been likened to anxiety disorders or body image disorders, it is more commonly regarded as an impulse-control disorder or BFRB – Body Focused Repetitive Behaviour. This means that a person is unable to stop themselves from carrying out a particular action, in this case hair pulling.

A person will experience a great urge to pull their hair out, with tension continuing to grow until the action is completed. Once the person has pulled a hair out, they feel a sense of relief from the built up tension or anxiety. This removal of hair often leads to very noticeable bald patches in sufferers of TTM, especially for those who focus on their scalp hair, eyelashes or eyebrows. TTM is not confined to the scalp, however, and it can apply to any body hair. Some people pull their eyebrows, eyelashes, or genital hair. Usually a person will pull hair using their fingers, but in other cases they may use tweezers or another hair removal device.

The reasons as to why sufferers pull their hair may differ depending on the situation or person. It is important to note that a person losing hair due to a skin infection is not suffering from TTM. The same is true if a person is removing hair due to a delusional thought or as a symptom of another condition, in which case they should seek immediate medical advice and treatment for their condition.

In cases of TTM, some people will pull their hair in response to a stressful or anxiety-provoking situation, which explains why TTM is sometimes regarded as an anxiety disorder. This is sometimes referred to as "focused hair pulling". Others may pull their hair in relaxed conditions, unaware they are, in fact, pulling at their hair. This is sometimes referred to as "automatic hair pulling."

A person is likely to partake in both focused and automatic hair pulling in different situations. In many cases, a person will not be able to describe the reason or trigger for pulling their hair. For some people, TTM is associated with negative emotions and is a response to negative feelings and events. In others, TTM is associated with positive emotions, such as the relief felt when hair is pulled.

What effects can trichotillomania have on a person?

As with all mental health problems, trichotillomania can greatly impact all aspects of a person's life. The negative feelings and emotions associated with TTM – including guilt – can heavily impact a sufferer's self-esteem. A sufferer can also feel embarrassed about losing their hair, attempt to conceal the condition and / or avoid social situations in which their hair loss may be noticed. This can be very isolating and badly affect their wellbeing – in some cases it can also lead to the development of other conditions, such as depression. This may partially explain why many sufferers of TTM also suffer from other mental health problems. Body image concerns are also likely to impact sufferers as a result of TTM, as having missing hair and bald spots may negatively impact the way a person views themselves.

Research has documented that trichotillomania can impact school and work performance as people may avoid attending due to feelings of embarrassment, or they may be unable to concentrate as a result of their urges, and concerns that people are judging their appearance. In some cases people may become angry or frustrated when fighting their urges, which can cause problems in the workplace. Some people unfortunately may turn to alcohol and illicit substances to try to help cope with these feelings; further impacting on their careers and causing additional problems with addiction and substance abuse.

There can also be physical health consequences of suffering from TTM. The most obvious physical consequence is the loss of hair and the potential for it to not regrow, leaving bald spots. There is however, a more dangerous physical health consequence of TTM; a subset of trichotillomania sufferers may chew on, or eat, their hair once they have pulled it out, known as trichophagia. While most people will accidentally swallow their hair at times in their life, the small quantity means this tends to be harmless. However, if a TTM sufferer is regularly pulling and swallowing hair, this can cause severe medical complications. Hair does not easily pass through the digestive system and instead becomes stuck. As more hair is swallowed, the hair sticks and balls together leading to a blockage known as a trichobezoar. This is extremely dangerous and will require surgery to be removed.

What causes trichotillomania?

As with most mental health conditions, researchers are yet to find a definitive cause of trichotillomania. Instead there are a number of theories regarding its causes. A number of theories tend to relate trichotillomania to other disorders and disorder groups, implying shared causation with other members of these disorder groups. For example, theories exist that suggest that TTM is an addiction, others suggest it is an expression of self-harm, and others suggest it may be a type of Obsessive Compulsive Disorder (OCD). In other cases it is said to be caused by underlying stress and anxiety, with hair pulling being used as a way to relieve this stress.

There are also theories that suggest that TTM relates to abuse, whereby those that have suffered abuse turn to hair pulling in order to appear less attractive and to confirm a negative self-view. While all these theories may have merit, they tend to suggest that TTM is the result of, or related to another condition, but we know this is not always the case.

When looking at TTM in isolation there are a number of theories that look at neurobiology and genetics. It has been theorised that there may be brain abnormalities in TTM sufferers, or that their genetics may be altered, with the hair pulling behaviours being inherited. Other theories focus on the age of onset, and suggest that hormonal changes may play a role in the onset of TTM. Others have taken note of some of the medications that may help relieve symptoms and have taken this to mean that lacking certain brain chemicals may result in TTM.

As you can see, there is no consensus in what causes TTM and more research in this area is definitely needed. It is likely that environmental factors as well as genetic factors will play a role in leading to TTM behaviours.

How many people are affected by trichotillomania?

Trichotillomania is an under-researched condition. While in recent years the research in the field has increased, there is still a vast gap in our knowledge of the disorder, and this includes our knowledge of its prevalence. Here we will discuss a few of the available statistics. It is worth noting that a number of these statistics are based on older classifications and so comparisons can be difficult. It is also important to remember that it is likely that a number of sufferers do not come forward and as such statistics are likely to be under representative.

Over the years there has been a change in the view of the mental health field regarding trichotillomania. While older studies from the 1960s tended to show that this was not a common disorder at all, suggesting only 0.05% of the population were affected[1], more recent studies have shown that the condition may be more common. The UK estimates for TTM have suggested that approximately 0.6% of the population is affected, which equalled over 370,000 people in 2009[2]. A number of American studies have supported this figure of 0.6%, using both college students[3] and the adult population[4]. Interestingly these studies also noted a higher rate of hair pulling that did not reach the diagnostic level of TTM. In fact one study found that, while 0.6% were suffering from TTM, 6.51% exhibited hair pulling behaviours, with 1.2% of the sample having clinically significant hair pulling behaviours[5]. In the college based sample it was found that hair pulling and hair loss at a non-diagnostic level impacted 1.5% of males and 3.4% of females[6]. Another study found that 1% to 3.5% of young adults and adolescents show clinically significant hairpulling[7]. A possible discrepancy appears here however, as one study is using a TTM diagnosis and the other claims significant hair pulling which may fall short of an official diagnosis.

Studies of psychiatric inmates suggesting a more conservative 4.4% lifetime prevalence, with a current rate of 3.4%[8], although these findings would be limited to those in psychiatric facilities who are already suffering from at least one other condition. Other researchers have chosen to look at hair loss or alopecia and found that, of their small sample of 59 children, 9.8% met criteria for TTM[9]. It is also important to highlight that this is a problem that is thought to greatly impact day-to-day life, with estimates suggesting that children and adolescents with TTM may spend between 30 and 60 minutes a day hair pulling, with much more time spent being distressed.

This is not just a problem seen in the UK and USA. One study out of Israel has found results that seem to align with those seen in the UK and USA, suggesting a lifetime prevalence rate of 1% in the adolescent population[10]. Polish researchers have also looked into the issue; instead of looking at those who are affected, these researchers contacted dermatologists. It was found that 68% of the dermatologists in the sample had seen a patient with TTM and 5% had seen 10 or more patients with TTM[11]. This highlights the ways in which people may be seeking help for a physical issue, potentially being unaware that the problem is based in mental health.

What treatments are available?

Unfortunately, as with most areas regarding trichotillomania, there has been little research done regarding successful treatment. Luckily, however, over the last few years research into TTM has gradually increased and this research has produced a number of potential treatment options, resulting in varying degrees of success.

It is important to remember that some people will respond better to some treatments better than others and in many cases treatments will be used in conjunction with each other. Ultimately, if you feel that you are suffering from TTM then it is important to seek professional treatment as soon as possible in order to have the best chance of successful treatment. TTM is a chronic condition, and although symptom severity may fluctuate over time, it is highly unlikely that symptoms will be reduced to a non-clinical level without treatment, but estimates suggest that at least 58% of people have never been treated for their condition[12]. The treatments likely to be offered can be broken down into medications and psychotherapies.

There are currently no medications that are specifically designed to target trichotillomania. However, medications designed for other conditions have been trialled and shown differing levels of success. For example, Selective Serotonin Reuptake Inhibitors (SSRIs) are usually used to treat Depression or Anxiety but have also been trialled in the treatment of TTM. Although SSRIs may still be trialled and used in treatment, especially when a person is presenting highly anxious or depressed alongside TTM symptoms, SSRIs are thought to not be effective at treating TTM symptoms. Another medication that may be used in the treatment of TTM is Clomipramine, which is another drug often used in the treatment of Depression and Obsessive Compulsive Disorder. Unlike SSRIs, Clomipramine has been shown to have some success in the treatment of hair pulling behaviours.

The most successful forms of treatment for trichotillomania are thought to be psychotherapies; more specifically Cognitive Behavioural Therapies (CBT), shown to have the most success when a person has a strong emotional support network. CBT helps a person change how they think and behave, by identifying the unhelpful thought patterns that a person has and how these affect behaviours. CBT may also result in reduced hair pulling behaviours and having people sit with the anxiety, highlighting that the anxiety or urge to hair pull will deplete over time. One popular form of CBT is Habit Reversal Training (HRT) which focusses on identifying the triggers that lead to hair pulling, such as increased periods of stress, which, once identified, can be replaced by alternative responses to such as clenching a fist. Emotional support is thought to be key in the successful treatment of TTM. Support can be drawn from friends or family, but in some cases people may find that these usual systems of support are not able to comprehend their feelings. In these situations a person may benefit from a self-help group, or an online forum. The Shaw Mind Foundation does provide a mental health forum where sufferers are able to look for support from other sufferers. Family therapy may also be useful not only in helping family members understand the problem of TTM, but it also in highlighting how a person's TTM might affect the rest of the family.

CBT treatment is thought to not only be successful in adults, but age appropriate CBT has also been shown to have some success in the treatment of trichotillomania in children. We strongly advise anybody who feels they are suffering from trichotillomania to seek professional help as soon as possible. The best way to seek treatment is via a General Practitioner who will be able to discuss any concerns. In many cases a person may be referred to a dermatologist first to ensure there is no physical basis for the irritation. They will then be referred to a psychologist or a psychiatrist to start their journey to recovery.

DERMATILLOMANIA / SKIN PICKING

What is dermatillomania?

Dermatillomania (DTM) is an impulse control disorder that involves the compulsion to pick at one's skin, resulting in wounding and damage. There are many different names for dermatillomania, in fact, while may people may refer to the disorder as dermatillomania, the official name is Excoriation Disorder. Other names include Skin picking disorder, pathological skin picking, and compulsive skin picking. All of these names refer to the same condition, which we will refer to as dermatillomania or DTM. Although skin picking behaviours have existed for many years, research into this area has been sparse, only picking up in recent years. In fact, DTM was only officially added as its own condition in the latest edition of the DSM-V.

It is important to realise that it is normal for people to occasionally pick at their skin. This only becomes a problem when it begins to cause distress, injury, or if it interferes with everyday life. For a person with DTM, there is often an extreme urge for them to pick their skin, with tension and distress building until they can complete the action. Once the skin picking has been completed, a person feels relieved and sometimes euphoric. The areas where a person picks can differ and be unique to the individual. For some sufferers, picking tends to focus on imperfections such as spots, moles, or previous scars or wounds. Others may pick at what they perceive to be imperfections, which are not noticeable to others, whereas others still may simply pick at an otherwise healthy piece of skin. This means that, while the facial area is often the most common site for skin picking, it can occur at any place on the body. Interestingly it is thought that sufferers will often change their picking site in order to let any wounds heal. In most cases people will pick using their finger nails and fingers, but some people do choose to use other methods to pick including biting or using external apparatus like scissors, pins or tweezers.

The reasoning behind picking may also differ between sufferers. Some sufferers will find that they pick in response to stressful or anxiety provoking situations, whereas others may skin-pick when they are bored. Others suggest that the picking gives them a sense of pleasure. In many cases people may not be able to identify why they skin-pick and in some cases a person may not be aware they have started to pick, and will instead skin-pick almost automatically. The rates in which people skin-pick is also likely to differ amongst sufferers. While some people may only skin-pick a few times a day, for a brief amount of time, others with more severe DTM may spend hours picking each day.

It is important to note that a diagnosis of DTM can only be made if other potential causes of the problem are ruled out. For example, there are a number of other mental health problems that may cause skin picking behaviours, such as Obsessive Compulsive Disorder, or Body Dysmorphic Disorder. There are also a number of physical health problems that cause skin irritations which can lead to scratching and picking, such as eczema. In these instances, while a person may be skin picking, they would not qualify for a diagnosis of dermatillomania.

What effects can dermatillomania have on a person?

As with all mental health problems, dermatillomania can greatly impact a person's life. Many people with DTM try to conceal their condition and will often avoid social settings so as to prevent others seeing their scars. This can be very isolating and can cause feelings of shame and guilt to manifest. The avoidance of others can also impact important social support networks, which can lead to other mental health problems associated with isolation. In some cases people will be so concerned about their condition they may avoid school or work which in turn will impact not only their future career, but can cause extreme financial hardship, leading to increased stress which may exacerbate their condition. For those who do attend school or work, the intense emotions caused by DTM can lead to conflict within these spaces, as well as potentially compromising friendships.

Having problems with skin picking may also lead to other mental health problems; findings suggest that those with dermatillomania have an increased risk of mood disorders like depression, anxiety disorders, and eating disorders[13]. It is also thought that males may show increased alcohol intake when they are suffering from skin picking[14]. It should be noted however that causation is not established and it may be that these conditions make a person more prone to skin picking, and not the other way around. Alarmingly there is also thought to be an increased risk of suicide in those who suffer with DTM, with some studies suggesting that 11.5% of sufferers will make an attempt on their own life[15]. If you are reading this and feel that you may be suicidal, we implore you to seek professional assistance immediately.

Dermatillomania does not only impact a person's mental wellbeing, it unsurprisingly has impacts on their physical health as well. Skin picking often leads to large areas of discolouration on a person's skin often resulting in scarring, with some severe instances requiring skin grafts. There are also situations where a person will pick deeper than the surface skin level and as such will cause deeper tissue problems. Next to the scarring are also problems with infection, where skin picking leaves open sores that then become infected. This can cause problems localised to the area, as well as with the whole body. In fact, there have been instances where bacteria was discovered in a person's blood as the result of DTM[16]; if left untreated these situations can become life threatening.

What causes dermatillomania?

While it is not known exactly what causes dermatillomania, there are a number of potential theories. A number of these suggest that dermatillomania is the result of other mental health problems, and as such shares causation with these disorders. Disorders and problems that have been linked to DTM include addiction, stress, and anxiety. There are also theories that DTM is not a standalone disorder but is instead a type of self-harm. Although it can be argued that the function of the behaviours differs too greatly for these problems to be related.

The development of acne as a teenager may play a part in DTM development. The majority of cases of DTM do begin around adolescence, the same time period where most cases of acne appear. It is therefore theorised that a person learns a behaviour regarding picking acne and simply continues to scratch and pick after the acne has cleared up. While this may initially seem like a promising cause, it does not explain why so many people who suffer from acne do not develop DTM, and why there are also cases of DTM first seen in later adulthood, long after acne is gone. Although it can be argued that onset at a later age is more likely to be related more to other skin conditions or stressful life events such as bereavement which are also theorised to be DTM triggers.

There has also been some support to suggest that there is an inherited component to DTM. One study found that, of those who screened positively for skin picking, a higher prevalence of skin picking was found in their immediate relatives[17]. A twin study has suggested that 40% of the variance in skin picking is due to genetic features, with the other 60% being due to non-shared environmental factors. The implications of this result clearly show that, as with many aspects of mental illness, the cause is likely rooted in an interaction between environmental and genetic factors.

How many people are affected by dermatillomania?

As dermatillomania is an under-researched topic, there is a limited amount of information regarding how many people are suffering. This is further hindered by the fact that misdiagnosis is likely to be high as this is a poorly understood condition; in fact one study has found that less than 20% of sufferers in a survey thought their clinician knew much about DTM[18]. Further problems are also found due to the tendency for people with DTM to conceal their condition.

This all combines to suggest that the true prevalence of the condition is likely to be much greater than the statistics discussed here. We should also note that comparing these statistics has its limitations as they are drawn from studies that use different classifications and diagnosis for DTM. However, it is the purpose of this section to give some idea of how much of a problem DTM truly is.

When looking at worldwide estimates, there is some suggestion that 2% to 3% of the population is suffering with dermatillomania[19]. Other estimates have varied slightly from this suggesting that the range of lifetime skin picking is more likely to be between 1.4% and 5.4% of the population, although this is not a worldwide estimate. One study that found that 1.4% of their sample satisfied criteria for DTM also found that 16.6% of their sample did show signs of skin picking that resulted in damage, with approximately 60% of these people being unable to explain this with another disorder. Of these people, 20–25% also reported feelings of distress and tension before picking. These findings highlight the fact that there are likely to be a number of people suffering as a result of skin picking behaviours, who may fall short of an official diagnosis. It is also important to note that many people who may show signs of skin picking are simply thought of as an annoying habit and do not cause distress.

In one study it was suggested that 3.8% of college students would meet diagnostic criteria for DTM[20].

Research on college students has not been confined to the USA. Results from around the globe show statistical differences but highlight how DTM is a problem that transcends cultures. In a small study from Pakistan it was found that 9% of the 210 students studied met criteria for DTM[21], a much higher statistic than what is often seen elsewhere.

A small Turkish study falls more in line with other findings, where 2% of the sample showed skin picking behaviours[22]. The number continues to climb in German research where a rate of 4.6% was found[23].

When looking at the age in which DTM may start, one study has suggested that the age of onset is often in childhood, finding that almost half of those interviewed showed skin picking behaviours prior to ten years of age[24]. Others have suggested a median age of onset of 30-45 years of age. It is always worth bearing in mind however, that this may simply highlight the different ways in which the disorder can impact people throughout their lifetimes.

What treatments are available?

Unfortunately, there has been limited research into the treatment of dermatillomania. However, there are treatments offered and these can be separated out into two main categories; medications and psychotherapies.

When looking at medications there is nothing specifically designed to treat dermatillomania. Instead, medications are borrowed from the treatments of other conditions such as depression and anxiety. One of the most commonly used medication groups are called Selective Serotonin Reuptake Inhibitors (SSRIs). While these drugs are the most regularly prescribed for treatment of DTM, unfortunately studies have tended to find that they are not greatly successful in reducing DTM symptoms[25]. This means that there is currently no medication that is reliably successful in the treatment of DTM. However, some sufferers may benefit from medications that alleviate some of their anxiety regarding their condition, or medications may be used for any conditions that are occurring alongside DTM, such as depression.

The most successful form of treatment for dermatillomania is psychotherapy – specifically Cognitive Behavioural Therapy (CBT), which increases in its utility if a sufferer has a strong emotional support network. The CBT used in the treatment of DTM will help to identify a person's negative thought patterns and will establish how these affect behaviours. It will likely also rely heavily on behavioural therapy, specifically Habit-Reversal Therapy (HRT). HRT first aims to help a person identify their triggers for picking, aiming to reduce skin picking behaviours by replacing these with less harmful behaviours.

Unfortunately there is a tendency for sufferers of dermatillomania to avoid seeking treatment, with some estimates suggesting that less than 20% of those with the condition seek help[26]. While we are aware that there are limited treatments available for DTM we do encourage anybody who is suffering to seek treatment for their condition and those conditions that may be occurring alongside DTM.

We hope this information has helped to increase knowledge and awareness of these two lesser researched conditions. If you do feel you are suffering with either condition then we encourage you to seek medical assistance and begin your road to recovery as soon as possible.

For more information on living with a mental health condition please visit our website: shawmindfoundation.org

Our forum where you can talk to others suffering from mental health concerns can be found here:

www.healthunlocked.com/mental-health-support

Written in July 2017 by Jack Ball

ACKNOWLEDGEMENTS

This little book was born during a time of isolation but as it has grown, so have the people I must thank.

To my editor, Stephanie at Trigger, for contacting me all those months ago with a view to publishing the book and making changes which have really given the book life.

To everyone else at Trigger, including the designers who made the most beautiful book cover and to Hannah, for listening to me, even when I had really silly questions (... and for letting me have red hair on the cover instead of brown)!

To my TSW family, for being the most extraordinary and inspirational community.

To my friends, for being there (even though for the most part they didn't have a clue I had trichotillomania and dermatillomania in the first place).

To my small but perfectly formed family, thank you.

To Mum, for everything.

If you found this book interesting …
why not read this next?

Geek Magnifique
Finding the Logic in my OCD

Feeling powerless against her OCD and emetophobia, Melissa suffered for years, until one day she decided to seek help and fully understand why her brain worked the way it did. Finding the logic in her OCD allowed her to take back control of her day-to-day life.

If you found this book interesting ...
why not read this next?

Must Try Harder

Adventures In Anxiety

After 30 years hiding in the shadows, beset by extreme social anxiety, Paula McGuire decided to change her worldview – one terrifying and exhilarating challenge at a time. In this book, Paula shares her extraordinary journey from recluse to adventurer.

REFERENCES

1   **Mansueto, C. S., & Rogers, K. E.** (2012). Trichotillomania: Epidemiology and Clinical Characteristics. In Grant, J. E., Stein, D. J., Woods, D. W., & Keuthen, N. J. (Eds.), *Trichotillomania, Skin Picking, and Other Body-Focused Repetitive Behaviors* (pp. 3-20). Arlington, VA: American Psychiatric Publishing, Inc.

2   **OCD UK** (nd.). *Trichotillomania* (TTM). Retrieved from: www.ocduk.org/trichotillomania

3   **Christenson, G. A., Pyle, R. L., & Mitchell, J. E.** (1991). Estimated lifetime prevalence of trichotillomania in college students. *The Journal of Clinical Psychiatry, 52,* 415-17.

4   **Duke, D. C., Bodzin, D. K., Tavares, P., Geffken, G. R., & Storch, E. A.** (2009). The phenomenology of hairpulling in a community sample. *Journal of Anxiety Disorders, 23,* 1118-125.

5   **Grant, J. E., Odlaug, B. L., & Chamberlain, S. R.** (2011). A cognitive comparison of pathological skin picking and trichotillomania. *Journal of Psychiatric Research, 45,* 1634-638.

6   **Christenson, G. A., Pyle, R. L., & Mitchell, J. E.** (1991). Estimated lifetime prevalence of trichotillomania in college students. *The Journal of Clinical Psychiatry, 52,* 415-17.

7   **Tolin, D. F., Diefenbach, G. J., Flessner, C. A., et al.** (2008). The Trichotillomania Scale for Children: Development and Validation. *Child Psychiatry to Human Development, 39,* 331-49.

8   Grant, J. E., Levine, L., Kim, D., & Potenza, M. N. (2005). Impulse control disorders in adult psychiatric inpatients. *The American Journal of Psychiatry, 162,* 2184-188.

9   Tolin, D. F., Franklin, M. E., Diefenbach, G. J., Anderson, E., & Meunier, S. A. (2007). Pediatric trichotillomania: descriptive psychopathology and an open trial of cognitive behavioural therapy. *Cognitive Behaviour Therapy, 36,* 129-44.

10 King, R. A., Zohar, A. H., Ratzoni, G., et al. (1995). An epidemiological study of trichotillomania in Israeli adolescents. *Journal of the American Academy of Child and Adolescent Psychiatry, 34,* 1212-215.

11 Szepietowski, J. C., Salomon, J., Pacan, P., Hrehorów, E., & Zalewska, A. (2009). Frequency and treatment of trichotillomania in Poland. *Acta Dermato-Venereologica, 89,* 267-70.

12 Lejoyeux, M., McLoughlin, M., & Adés, J. (2000). Epidemiology of behavioral dependence: literature review and results of original studies. *European Psychiatry, 15,* 129-34.

13 Leibovici, V., Murad, S., Cooper-Kazaz, R., et al. (2014). Excoriation (skin picking) disorder in Israeli University students: prevalence and associated mental health correlates. *General Hospital Psychiatry, 36,* 686-89.

14 Odlaug, B. L., Lust, K., Schrieber, L. R., et al. (2013). Skin picking disorder in university students: health correlates and gender differences. *General Hospital Psychiatry, 35,* 168-73.

15 SkinPick. (nd.). *Everything you need to know about Dermatillomania.* Retrieved from: www.skinpick.com/dermatillomania

16 Hawatmeh, A., & Al-khateeb, A. (2017). An unusual complication of dermatillomania. *Quantitative Imaging in Medicine and Surgery, 7,* 166-68.

17 Monzani, B., Rijsdijk, F., Cherkas, L., et al. (2012). Prevalence and Heritability of Skin Picking in an Adult

Community Sample: A Twin Study. *American Journal of Medical Genetics, 159B,* 605-10.

18 **Tucker, B. T. P., Woods, D. W., Flessner, C. A., Franklin, S. A., & Franklin, M. E.** (2011). The Skin Picking Impact Project: Phenomenology, interference, and treatment utilization of pathological skin picking in a population-based sample. *Journal of Anxiety Disorders, 25,* 88-95.

19 **Keuthen, N. J., Koran, L. M., Aboujaoude, E., Large, M. D., & Serpe, R. T.** (2010). The prevalence of pathologic skin picking in US adults. *Comprehensive Psychiatry, 51,* 183-86.

20 **Keuthen, N.J., Deckersbach, T., Wilhelm, S., et al.** (2000). Repetitive skin picking in a student population and comparison with a sample of self-injurious skin-pickers. *Psychosomatics, 41,* 210-15.

21 **Siddiqui, E. U., Maeem, S. S., Naqvi, H., & Ahmed, B.** (2012). Prevalence of body-focused repetitive behaviors in three large medical colleges of Karachi: a cross-sectional study. *BMC Research Notes, 5,* 614. http://doi.org/10.1186 /1756-0500-5-614

22 **Calikusu, C., Kucukgoncu, S., Tecer, O., & Bestepe, E.** (2012). Skin picking in Turkish students: prevalence, characteristics, and gender differences. *Behavior modification, 36,* 49-66.

23 **Bohne, A., Wilhelm, S., Keuthen, N. J., Baer, L., & Jenike, M. A.** (2002). Skin picking in German students: Prevalence, phenomenology, and associated characteristics. *Behavior Modifications, 26,* 320-339.

24 **Odlaug, B. L., & Grant, J. E.** (2007). Childhood-onset pathologic skin picking: clinical characteristics and psychiatric comorbidity. *Comprehensive Psychiatry, 48,* 388-93.

25 **Schumer, M. C., Bartley, C. A., & Bloch, M. H.** (2016). Systematic Review of Pharmacological and Behavioral Treatments for Skin Picking Disorder. *Journal of Clinical Psychopharmacology, 36,* 147-52.

26 Grant, J. E., Odlaug, B. L., Chamberlain, S. R., et al. (2012). Skin Picking Disorder. *The American Journal of Psychiatry, 169,* 1143-149.

the *Shaw* mind
FOUNDATION

Creating hope for children,
adults and families

Sign up to our charity, The Shaw Mind Foundation
www.shawmindfoundation.org
and keep in touch with us; we would love to hear
from you.

*We aim to bring to an end the suffering and despair caused
by mental health issues. Our goal is to make help and support
available for every single person in society, from all walks of
life. We will never stop offering hope. These are our promises.*

www.triggerpublishing.com

Trigger is a publishing house devoted to opening conversations about mental health. We tell the stories of people who have suffered from mental illnesses and recovered, so that others may learn from them.

Adam Shaw is a worldwide mental health advocate and philanthropist. Now in recovery from mental health issues, he is committed to helping others suffering from debilitating mental health issues through the global charity he co-founded, The Shaw Mind Foundation. www.shawmindfoundation.org

Lauren Callaghan (CPsychol, PGDipClinPsych, PgCert, MA (hons), LLB (hons), BA), born and educated in New Zealand, is an innovative industry-leading psychologist based in London, United Kingdom. Lauren has worked with children and young people, and their families, in a number of clinical settings providing evidence based treatments for a range of illnesses, including anxiety and obsessional problems. She was a psychologist at the specialist national treatment centres for severe obsessional problems in the UK and is renowned as an expert in the field of mental health, recognised for diagnosing and successfully treating OCD and anxiety related illnesses in particular. In addition to appearing as a treating clinician in the critically acclaimed and BAFTA award-winning documentary *Bedlam*, Lauren is a frequent guest speaker on mental health conditions in the media and at academic conferences. Lauren also acts as a guest lecturer and honorary researcher at the Institute of Psychiatry Kings College, UCL.

Please visit the link below:

www.triggerpublishing.com

Join us and follow us...

@triggerpub

Search for us on Facebook